The Mass and the Interior Life

The Mass
AND THE
Interior Life

BERNARDO
VASCONCELOS, OSB

Originally published in Portuguese as
A Missa e a Vida Interior in 1936.

First Published in English under the title *Your Mass* by
Scepter Publishers LTD., Dublin 1960
Second Edition © by Arouca Press, 2021

Nihil Obstat: Msgr. T. F. O'Reilly, V. Gen.

Imprimi Potest: ✠ Joannes Carolus, Archiep. Dublinen.,
Hierniae Primas.

Dublini die 22 Augusti 1960.

All rights reserved:
No part of this book may be reproduced or transmitted,
in any form or by any means, without permission

ISBN: 978-1-989905-36-4 (pbk)
ISBN: 978-1-989905-37-1 (hardcover)

Arouca Press
PO Box 55003
Bridgeport PO
Waterloo, ON N2J3G0
Canada
www.aroucapress.com
Send inquiries to info@aroucapress.com

Book and cover design
by Michael Schrauzer

CONTENTS

FOREWORD ix
PREFACE xi

1 I Will Go In Unto the Altar of God 1
2 I Have Sinned Exceedingly 7
3 Lord, Have Mercy On Us 15
4 Glory Be To God On High 19
5 Good News 25
6 A Host for a Host 33
7 Actio I: The Preface 41
8 Actio II: The Canon 45
9 Actio III: The Consecration 53
10 Actio IV: Doxology 61
11 The Kiss of Peace 71
12 Kiss of Love: Communion 75
13 Thanksgiving 97

About the Author 103

FOREWORD

'THE APOSTLE'S EXHORTATION "YOURS IS TO BE THE mind that Christ showed" requires all Christians, as far as human power allows, to reproduce in themselves the sentiments which Christ had when He was offering Himself in sacrifice.'

These words of Pope Pius XII in his encyclical letter *Mediator Dei*[1] had not appeared when the holy author of this book died in 1932. Yet the same fundamental idea runs through his book. The author sets out to show how the sacrifice of the Mass demands an active participation by the faithful, who should be co-offerers and co-victims with Christ in it, and how the spirit of the sacrifice should permeate their whole life and work. His method is not that of one exposing abstract doctrine, but of a teacher who carefully analyses the familiar prayers and texts of the Mass itself. Each meditation begins with a text, such as the *Confiteor* or *Sanctus*, which is only too familiar to the average Catholic, and after a careful exposition of all that it contains and suggests, the author links it to the daily lives of his readers, challenging them or exhorting them to mould their lives in accordance with its spirit and teaching. By this means their worship of God at Mass will be more genuine, and during the day they will 'live' the Mass.

1 no. 85.

PREFACE

THE EUCHARIST, SAYS SAINT THOMAS, IS A *SACRIFICE* in as much as we offer it and a *sacrament* in as much as we eat it.

Unfortunately, many of the faithful have lost all appreciation of that intimate relationship between the Mass and Communion; they dissociate the sacrament from the sacrifice. But we never have, indeed we cannot have, the sacrament without the sacrifice.

In fact, from the dogmatic, liturgical and ascetical points of view, the sacrifice is the essence of the Eucharist; and on the other hand, the Communion is an *integral* part of the holy Mass. So that the holy Sacrifice would be incomplete if it had not at least one communicant, the priest. Consequently those who live the *sacrament* of the Eucharist should also live the *sacrifice*, which is its principle and its source; they should integrate the former with the latter, at least *intentionally*.

And if they do not *live* the sacrifice of the Eucharist, they easily forget the active part which they should take in the holy Mass, as co-offerers and co-victims.

This is such an enormous loss to their spiritual life that it is hardly surprising if they lack that special veneration and affection which they ought to have for the holy Sacrifice; it is no wonder they care little whether they receive holy Communion at Mass or outside Mass; no wonder that, to some degree at least, they separate their interior life from the holy Mass.

Now, since there can be no sacrament of the Eucharist without the sacrifice of the Eucharist, those who live by the former must live by the latter, which is its source.

That is to say: we must *live* the holy Mass. The holy Mass is the centre around which the whole liturgy revolves. And the liturgy is the primary and indispensable source of the true Christian spirit.

Consequently the Mass must be the *centre* of every perfect Christian life. This life is called *interior* in as much as it is hidden with Christ in God.

The Mass must therefore be the *centre of all our interior life*.

THESE PAGES, NOW COLLECTED IN ONE SMALL VOLume, have been written for the purpose of helping the faithful, ordinary souls, to attain one most important object: active participation in the holy Sacrifice of the Mass; so that, consciously and deliberately, they may offer the sacred Victim, offer themselves and be nourished by receiving the holy Eucharist. In a word: that they may live the blessed Eucharist, the sacrifice and the sacrament, in its entirety, and that by living it they may sanctify themselves more and more, for that is the will of God: *Haec est voluntas Dei, sanctificatio vestra* (I Thess. IV, 3).

THE FIRST THREE CHAPTERS—*I WILL GO IN UNTO the altar of God*; *I have sinned exceedingly*; *Lord, have mercy on us*—are intended to arouse in us heartfelt *sorrow for our sins*, an indispensable basis of the spiritual edifice. Only thus can we say that it is founded on a firm rock.

That is the *purgative way*.

Then the soul contemplates, praises, blesses, entreats and adores the Lord—in the *Gloria*—makes sincere and holy resolutions to follow him to the end—*Good News*—and offers itself with him as a victim—*A host for a host*. Enraptured, it goes on to sing his perfections, all his attributes, especially his holiness. And it never tires of repeating that he is holy, holy, holy—*Preface*.

Then comes all that mysterious conversation which is the Canon. The heart opens out in prayer for the Church militant and suffering, and in commemoration of the Church triumphant.

The moment of the Consecration is a most solemn one, the most majestic moment of the Mass.

A few words from the priest and...God obeys.

And the soul contemplates Jesus, present there on the altar.

It prostates itself in adoration and, enlightened by grace, acknowledges that it is through him, with him and in him that all honour and glory is given to the Father, in the unity of the holy Ghost—*Per ipsum.*

This is contemplation: the *contemplative way*, the purest and loftiest of prayers.

And then the soul, all bathed in divine light, feels a generous desire to give itself to others, to become all things to all men—*The kiss of peace.* It enters into union, into Communion, with its God—*The kiss of love.*

This is the *unitive way.*

Finally it gives thanks, sincere thanks, for the many benefits received.

All its life is an unceasing act of gratitude—*Thanksgiving*—and at the same time a continual preparation for a more and more intimate union with the divine Spouse.

IN WRITING THESE PAGES, I HAVE BEEN INSPIRED by a heartfelt desire to do something for the good of souls: to make the holy Mass better known and consequently more deeply loved and lived, for it is the centre of all our worship, the soul of our religion, the complete programme of our sanctity and a wonderful summary of dogma and morals. If I succeed in this I shall have co-operated in spreading the kingdom of God among men and disposed recognition of God's rights over their lives.

Bernardo Vasconcelos

I
I Will Go In Unto the Altar of God

GOD WANTS US TO BE SAINTS! HE DESIRES OUR sanctity because he loves us infinitely, and we should desire it with him. He wants to make us saints, to make us participate and share in his own life; for that purpose, he adopts us as his children and heirs to his infinite glory. But God adopts us as his children only through his Son, Jesus Christ; it is in him and through him that God wants to be united with us, and us to be united with him.

Christ is the way, the way which can lead us to God; without him we can do nothing.

We shall be saints only in so far as the life of Jesus Christ is in us. Interior life consists in this. The gospel very often speaks to us of Christ's interior life: he passed whole nights in prayer; to Mary and Joseph who had been looking for him, full of fear and sorrow, he answered: 'Did you not know that I must be about my Father's business?'

Jesus is our model: we must imitate him. So we also must live an interior life.

You too, my friend, must try to have an interior life.

If you live in the cloister and have no interior life, you belie the life which you profess; you lie to God and to men.

If you live in the middle of the world, you must make every effort possible to live this life more and more intensely: it is indispensable to the progress of your soul. Perhaps in your present circumstances this is not—or does not seem to be—a very easy task. It may be because you are still very attached to all kinds of evil, and consequently incapable of intensifying the life of grace in your soul: in that case you must try from now on to remove all these obstacles; it may be because the duties of your state in life absorb your attention and sap your energy in such a way that it is—or seems to be—very difficult for you, in the few free moments of your day, to live that intimate relationship with the divine Spouse.

Yes, to live an interior life may not seem very easy to you in these circumstances; but in fact it is not difficult at all.

In the first place, you must accustom yourself, as someone has said, to 'waste time' praying: afterwards you will find that you have new powers of concentration, a new capacity for hard work, which will enable you to do more and do it well. Secondly, even in the middle of the tasks of each busy day, there is no one who cannot, if he wants to, raise his heart to God from time to time.

If you want to go to him with all the earthiness of your soul, and if you try to reach him with all your heart, not only will you find it easy to invoke him and remember him from time to time, you will even find it necessary, time and again, to glance at him with the eyes of your soul.

PERHAPS UP TO THIS YOU HAVE NOT THOUGHT seriously of interior life, maybe because you looked on it as something which you had no right to desire, because it is granted only to a few chosen ones, and you did not count yourself one of these.

Well look, my dear friend: you also must desire and try to acquire that interior life. Aim at it from this moment on, as an unquestionable truth, and begin *now* to prepare yourself to live it as well as possible. Perhaps it may be a revelation for you, a new world, as it has been for so many other souls.

From then on you will notice a great sense of wonder, great enthusiasm, a thousand and one energies awakening in you,—in a word: a new life in your soul.

Wonder and enthusiasm, yes, like someone who thinks that the world ends over here, just at those distant mountains, where the sky fades away and the horizon seems to unfold everything... and then one day from the top of those same mountains he sees new lands, an endless ocean, a new sky, a new horizon stretching as far as the eye can see. Then will you say: I too can travel through these lands, over those new seas, and contemplate those undreamed of skies... I too can live that new life which up to now the eyes of my soul had never seen...

But this is something great, something marvelous!

Yes, my friend, you can walk these ways with confidence.

It is extraordinary, it is sublime, that God himself should want to live with us, should deign to live *in us*! But it is a fact; it is reality. Try to live that reality more and more; drench, saturate, drown your soul in it. Come, my friend, come. It is not I, poor sinner, it is he himself who calls you. 'You are to be prefect, as your heavenly Father is perfect' (Mt. V, 48).

Open wide your heart and be docile to his action, which will make a saint of you. You too are called to have a mystical knowledge of God; that is a knowledge to which *all* the faithful *must* aspire.

We all can and must prepare ourselves to receive that favour from God, although we can never reach it unaided.

Do you want to know how to prepare yourself to receive that unextraordinary, but very excellent grace?

Look: what you have to do, as Canon Saudreau says, is to avoid sin, which deforms nature; exercise the faculties of the soul and prepare them, by means of prayer, for the grace which reforms it; by holy conduct, for the justice which purifies it; by meditation, for the knowledge which illuminates it; by contemplation, for the wisdom which brings perfection.

JUST AS THE WHOLE OF JESUS' LIFE CONVERGED and tended towards the Cross—and it was from his preview of Calvary and its fruits, so to speak, that he got his strength and encouragement—so too our whole life must converge and tend towards the unbloody renewal of the Sacrifice of the Cross, the holy Mass; it must be a continuous preparation and, at the same time, an unceasing act of thanksgiving for that Sacrifice; it is from our *active participation* in the holy Mass that we must draw new strength and new vigour.[1]

IF ONLY WE *LIVED* THE HOLY MASS!

If only we assisted at that sublime Sacrifice in union with holy Church, praying as she teaches us to pray; if only we united ourselves to Jesus' sacrifice and sacrificed ourselves with him; if only we offered up to God the Father, in union with the Son in whom he is well pleased, all the sufferings, self-denials and tribulations of each day; in a word, if we took an active part in the holy Sacrifice: then our sufferings would not be wasted, for the Lord would unite them with his own passion, and would give us a share in that glory which God the Father conferred on his own sacred Humanity in return for all his sufferings. Besides all that, they would be a fruitful source of glory for the elect, of merit for the just, of pardon for sinners and of relief from their pains for the souls in purgatory.

MY FRIEND, HOW I WISH YOU WOULD LIVE THE holy Mass; that, in spite of all your occupations and the duties of your state in life, your whole day should be a continuous preparation for the holy Sacrifice and at the same time a never-ending act of thanksgiving.

For a soul in the state of grace all actions can be prayer.

A continuous preparation! For we are miserable creatures whereas the Sacrifice is most excellent and the Victim is thrice holy.

A never-ending act of thanksgiving! Because we must never forget the innumerable benefits we receive from the

---

[1] 'In the precious death of thy just ones, O Lord, (this refers particularly to the holy martyrs Cosmas and Damian, patrons of the stational church) we offer to thee that sacrifice from which martyrdom received its very beginning': *Secret of Thursday of the third week in Lent.*

Lord, which are all summarized and contained in this mysterious renewal of the Sacrifice of the Cross; and because, in any case, we will never be able to give him sufficient thanks for those graces whose real value we will never appreciate properly until this life ends.

I should like you to *live* the holy Mass. It is because I desire that so much, and with the sole aim of helping you, that I have written these pages.

11
I Have Sinned Exceedingly

WHEN WE CONFESS OUR SINS, PROVIDED WE HAVE true contrition, by that very act we give glory to God. But if we confess them as a matter of routine, without fully realizing what we are saying, then we do not give him any glory.

I know that anything which is repeated many times becomes less perfect day by day, out of sheer habit. I know we are so weak that this happens even in holy things. But look: if you want—and you must want—to react against that loss of vitality which comes from frequent recital of these prayers, then try, with great love, to go deeper and deeper into their meaning, and look for practical applications of that meaning.

YOU WILL NOTICE THAT THE PRIEST HUMILIATES himself many times during Mass. 'I have sinned exceedingly, by thought, word and deed...' Here the Church obliges him to acknowledge publicly, in the presence of the Church triumphant and militant, and especially before the faithful who are present, that he is a sinner.

There he is, asking to be purified of his iniquities, so that he may be allowed to enter with the pure spirits into the Holy of Holies. He hopes to be pardoned of his sins through the merits of the saints whose relics are in the altar on which he is about to celebrate the holy Sacrifice.

After reading a passage of the gospel[1] he prays: 'By the words of the gospel may our sins be blotted out.'

At the Offertory he acknowledges that he is an unworthy servant of the heavenly Father, unworthy to offer him the immaculate Host for his 'countless sins, offences and

---

[1] Except in *Requiem* Masses.

negligences, for all here present; as also for all faithful Christians, living and dead.'

And it is 'in a spirit of humility and with a contrite heart' that he asks to be received by the Lord.

Almost at the conclusion of the Canon he strikes his breast and, remembering the Church suffering, militant and triumphant, asks that sinners should be given a share in the inheritance and fellowship of the holy apostles and martyrs.

Before receiving the Lord in holy Communion, he asks him in the *Our Father*: 'forgive us our trespasses as we forgive them who trespass against us.'

Again, when he prepares to unite himself with Jesus, he asks him to regard not his sins, but the merits and faith of his Church.

He then gives the kiss of peace to the ministers[2] and asks the Lord Jesus to deliver him by his most holy body and blood from all his transgressions and from all evils, and that his reception of the body of the Lord Jesus Christ should not turn to his judgement and condemnation.

The moment of the Communion is approaching. And then the priest, looking lovingly at the sacred Host which he holds in his hands, repeats the words of the centurion, who by his faith and humility obtained a cure for his son: 'Lord, I am not worthy that thou shouldst enter under my roof; say but the word and my soul shall be healed.'

Notice that the Church commands *all* priests to pronounce these words, even if they are saints!

It is true that Jesus' sacrifice in itself is always acceptable to his Father in heaven. But in so far as that sacrifice is offered by us, it will be acceptable only on condition that our soul be filled with a deep sense of sorrow and great humility.

Besides, as Saint John says: 'If we say that we have no sin, the truth is not in us.'

---

2   In solemn Masses.

THE HOLY CHURCH IS VERY WISE IN OBLIGING priests to make so many acts of sorrow and humility during the Mass. For 'if, when we wish to obtain some favour from those who have the power to help us, we dare not ask except with humility and reverence, how much more reason is there that we should present our petitions to the Lord God of the universe in all lowliness of heart and purity of devotion.'[3]

In fact, if the priest is well penetrated with the sublime dignity of his functions, if he fully realizes their greatness, how can he but acknowledge his nothingness in the eyes of the Lord of all things?

HOW CAN HE BE ANYTHING BUT CONFUSED AT THAT unheard-of marvel, and not, in its light, see more clearly his own miseries, his nothingness—feel the necessity of humiliating himself, of proclaiming his faults publicly?

And what a beautiful prayer that acknowledgement of our faults is! How appropriately it proclaims the power, the holiness of God, and calls down his graces on us! For 'one abyss calls upon another.'[4]

LOOK, MY FRIEND: DO NOT BE SURPRISED TO SEE that many souls that are deeply religious and consecrated to God have, at times, a very unstable spiritual life, and are subject to a thousand fluctuations which unceasingly oppose their interior progress, seeking to impede their advancement on the road to heaven.

If you look carefully you will find that, more often than not, the cause of this tremendous hesitation is lack of sorrow, that most sure means of averting sin, of setting one's spiritual life on a solid and stable basis.

The greatest saints never ceased to foster and advocate this most holy interior disposition. In their souls it was something much greater than a series of isolated acts or passing

---

3 Rule of St. Benedict, chapter XX.
4 St. Francis de Sales: *Letter to Madame de Chantal*, 2 December, 1609.

impulses. The expressions of deep sorrow which they often uttered were nothing more than the outward signs of a permanent and stable inward attitude eager to find an outlet.

Indeed, God's generosity towards these great souls makes them acknowledge all the more sorrowfully the enormity of their ingratitude towards him. In the splendor of the divine light, the slightest fault seems an enormous crime... So, my friend, we should always live in a state of repentance, until the last moment of our life, and not let even one day pass without trying to blot out our faults with tears of sorrow. Is it not true that we forget our miseries very quickly, with a levity at times quite frightening?

I do not ask you, far from it, to think of them all the time, so that they become an obsession with you, sapping all your healthy energies. No, but lament them every day in your prayer, in a general way, without trying to remember particular instances: for this would only weaken your true repentance. Then, lift up your eyes to the Lord of mercy...

Would it not be a very good thing to ask pardon for your faults precisely during those moments when the *Confiteor* is being said at the foot of the altar, genuinely convinced that you too contributed to the passion of your Lord; and to humiliate yourself, like the priest and with the priest, every time he humiliates himself during the Mass?

THERE ARE SOME SOULS WHO MAKE THEMSELVES martyrs by thinking too much, and in an unhealthy way, of all the trivial details of the sins they have committed, as if they were anxious to discover material to torment themselves anew; and finally, instead of reacting and adopting a new method, they fall prey to discouragement, which does not come from God.

Never let me see you act thus.

Never lose confidence in the Lord's mercy. Remember that the expiation and the merits of Christ have an infinite value, that he is still alive and intercedes for us.

True sorrow brings great peace to the soul.

If you have a tendency to that discouragement — in some souls it is almost a permanent state — and if even consideration of the Lord's infinite mercy does not bring peace to your distressed soul, then bring to memory, but with great humility, the good works of your past life.

HAVE YOU NEVER SEEN SOULS, WHO LIVE AN APPARently good spiritual life, falling into grave sin?

The reason is that these souls reject the inspirations and the action of the holy Ghost time after time; they offend frequently and deliberately against humility, charity, obedience... They are full of themselves, very attached to their own opinion, in short, very wrapped up in themselves.

The holy Ghost is then grieved; he calls no more on those souls but goes away in silence.

One day in these souls the wind of temptation will blow more strongly. A soul that was loyal and receptive to the inspirations of the holy Ghost, would resist it perfectly, with the help of the Lord. But these poor souls fall down defeated, victims of their own lack of generosity towards God and of their selfishness, which is the source of their infidelities and of their deliberate faults.

If those souls were touched by the spirit of remorse, if they were in a state of habitual contrition, they would certainly not fall thus, because remorse is essentially opposed to deliberate sin.

That sentiment would make them strong against temptation, which God permits only for our greater good; it would foster in their souls an aversion to sin; it would put them on their guard against the snares of the enemy.

LOOK, MY FRIEND: CONTRITION IMPRINTS ON our whole life a certain religious gravity, and removes all levity of spirit.

And thus, if the eyes of our soul are fixed on God above

all other things, that is to say, if the soul is habitually penetrated with fear of God—the fountain of wisdom—we shall live an interior life full of holy gravity, which will prepare us in an excellent manner for great spiritual progress. For 'the more a man's practical life is penetrated with the divine idea, the more he progresses in understanding his own dependence and nothingness! His obedience will become more profound and he will abandon himself more completely into the arms of God's paternal love.'[5]

A SPIRIT OF PENANCE AND JOY...

For some souls these two seem incompatible: they look on penance as something dull, boring, gloomy... And, since the spiritual life can be stable and secure only when it is solidly based on penance, they regard religion as something very sad; they are not willing to take up their sweet yoke; rather, they have not the courage to break away from the heavy and enslaving yoke of their passions; they do not want to put an end to *their pleasures*. Yes, *their* pleasures: all based on dissipation, all superficial, exterior and unsatisfying. The truth is, they know nothing of genuine Christian joy 'calm and profound, sincere and true, constant and persevering; that joy of which our Lord told the apostles: "Your joy no man shall take from you"; joy of spirit and heart; joy of soul; pure in its origin, beneficial in its effects; joy which comes from God and leads to him, and which is the sense of the presence of God in us.'[6]

Those people do not know what it is to forget themselves; their soul is never free from the oppressing weight of the consciousness of their own *ego*, of their personal needs. They never think of others. Perhaps they might even be scandalized if we asked them to share, to be concerned with, the difficulties of others, out of love for them; if we told them

---

5 D. I Ryelandt: *Eassai sur la physionomie morale de Saint Benoît*, Chapter III, II.
6 Mgr. de Gibergues: *Entretiens sur l'Eucharistie*.

that, because it would open their heart, their own sufferings would be alleviated. No, they know nothing of love. They have no idea how to love. Love transforms sacrifices into joys: when we love, in every cross we see Jesus, and we love it because we love him. Let us ask God to make us love every cross.

IF CONTRITION OF HEART IS SUCH A PRECIOUS VIRtue, so much fostered and advocated by the greatest saints; if it brings religious gravity and stability to our interior life; if it brings peace to our soul; if it brings to our heart confidence, charity and that holy joy of the just: why should we not ask the Lord for it, as one of his greatest graces? Why should we not arouse and awaken it within ourselves by meditating on the passion of the Lord, in the Way of the Cross? Why do we not join with the celebrant in all those expressions of repentance which the holy Church puts at his disposal? My friend, let us do so from today on. Let us commence at once.

III

Lord, Have Mercy On Us

LORD, HAVE MERCY ON US! THIS IS THE CRY UTTERED by the ten lepers in Palestine when the Saviour was passing.

All of us, poor sinners, are covered in sores, rotting with leprosy, maimed and half blind. Let us show our sores to the Lord; let us uncover our wounds completely in his divine presence, like those poor men who sit begging at the side of the road whenever a crowd is passing.

Lord, have mercy on us.

Who can help us better than he?

LET US DO MORE. LET US SHOW TO THE FATHER OF heaven the five wounds of his Son, like a banner of peace, peace which our soul so much desires, like a banner of glory...

What a treasure we have in those five wounds!

Those wounds were inflicted for love of us, for love of you, my friend, whoever you may be.

Every time you contritely bring to mind the fact that you contributed to the Lord's death, remember too that his wounds are worth more than all the treasures in the world, and raise up your heart in an act of thanksgiving.

They were inflicted, as Saint Augustine mentions somewhere, so that we can make our way into them and find rest there from the labours of our long exile...

They are an oasis in this great desert, a light in the darkness of this dusky world.

LOOK FOR A MOMENT AT GOD'S OWN INTIMATE life...He enjoys the fullness of life. What good can the creation of man do him? Nevertheless he decrees that creatures be called to participate in his own divine life. Because of his enormous love, he pours out his life on us, mere creatures called out of nothing into existence. Thus we are raised high above our own nature. And then God goes further: he makes of these mere creatures, and names them, his own sons. They are the offspring, the children, of his love.

This decree becomes a reality in Adam. Adam sins and, in his disgrace, drags down with him all his posterity. And then that decree, violated so outrageously, is restored by a marvelous invention of justice, mercy and goodness.

God so loved men that he gave them his own only begotten Son... The word of God became flesh in order to be the Way... And *his own* knew him not! And *we* know him not!

Jesus becomes a host because he loves us. A host so great that it unites earth and heaven... A host so small that it can be held between a man's fingers... And we leave him alone in his sacrifice! We have no wish to be hosts like him!

Lord have mercy on us!

WE ARE SURPRISED THAT THOSE TWO DISCIPLES AS they were going along the road to Emmaus on the day of the resurrection, did not recognize the Lord who was walking at their side and talking to them... Yet how often do we fail to recognize—and even deny—the Lord in the many difficulties which come to us in a thousand different ways? We fail to recognize him in our own suffering brothers, in our poor, in all those to whom the world is unkind.

Lord, have mercy on us!

THE LORD HAS UNITED HIMSELF MYSTICALLY WITH our soul, in a manner comparable, but far superior, to the bond of marriage.

He has called us for himself, he has attracted us to his heart, so as to make us one with himself... But we go our way along other paths, seeking other unions, attaching our heart to a thousand passing things...

Christ, have mercy on us.

WHAT WONDER THAT THE PRIEST SHOULD FEEL confused on entering the Holy of Holies! He has been raised to the highest dignity on this earth and he lives, perhaps, very close to the shadows of death, or even enveloped in them.

And on seeing shadows all about him, on seeing that everything is darkness, he cannot but repeat, very often, this cry of the lepers:

Christ, have mercy on us!

AND YOU, MY FRIEND, WHO ACCOMPANY THE PRIEST, reading the Mass devoutly in your missal; you who are going to be united to Jesus in holy Communion; you who are also surrounded by shadows: do you not feel the same desire to cry out:

Christ, have mercy on us?

YOU KNOW WELL THAT WE ARE ALL MEMBERS OF the one mystical Body of the Church, whose head is Jesus Christ. All men are brothers in Christ. To hurt one of our brothers is to hurt Jesus himself.

If we thought often enough about this, if we *lived* this marvelous principle of unity, how many offences against charity we could avoid! Let us resolve from this moment on to be 'all things to all men' (I Cor. IX, 22), with the holy purpose of saving them all.

What an enormous amount of good we can do for our brothers—at least for those with whom we live! One thing we can do, and must do, is to pray for them all, without any exception. Ah, if only we had faith in the value of prayer, a living faith, and blind to all the fluctuations and vanities of this world, deaf to all those suggestions which come from the 'prudence of the flesh,' quick to resist every sign of distrust in the Lord's promises.

But no. We are men 'of little faith.' Let us at least acknowledge the fact and ask the Lord to increase our faith.

So let us say from the bottom of our heart:

Lord, have mercy on us.

WE ARE ALWAYS QUICK TO ASK FOR FAVOURS, SO let us be equally quick to thank the Lord when he grants them. Notice that of the ten lepers miraculously cured, only one returned to thank the Lord! We are the other nine, the ungrateful. As if our life were not meant to be—as it can be—one unceasing act of thanksgiving: souls in the state of grace, a pure life, a light always burning in the temple of the soul, an imperfect temple indeed, but one in which the blessed Trinity dwells.

Ah, if only we thought about that! What precious gifts the Lord has given us and allows us to keep within ourselves, for we are *temples of God*.

But also how fragile are the vessels in which we carry these gifts! Let us, then, be aware of our incomparable dignity... but also of our unequalled weakness. May the consciousness of so many gifts and the fear of losing them all make us whisper to the Lord, very, very often:

Lord, have mercy on us.

THE HUMBLE CONFESSION OF OUR FAULTS, OF OUR nothingness, glorifies God immensely, exalts his omnipotence and his holiness. To acknowledge our own lowliness is to ascend on high. Our eyes, cast down to the earth, bring God down from heaven.

Let us, then, say with the priest:

Lord, have mercy on us.

IV

Glory Be To God On High

THIS HYMN, TO WHICH WE APPLY THE EPITHET 'angelic' because of the opening words, is a liturgical pearl dating perhaps from the second century of Christianity.[1] Originally it belonged to the liturgy of matins or dawn. Later, probably after the second century,[2] it was placed in the position which it occupies today in the Roman liturgy, that is, between the *Kyrie* and the Collects of the Mass. At the beginning of the sixth century Pope Symmachus decreed that this hymn should be recited on Sundays and on the feasts of martyrs. But this decree applied only to bishops; priests could recite it only on Easter Sunday. On days on which there was a station, or on which Mass was preceded by a procession, the *Gloria* was omitted even in the papal Mass.

Little by little the priests began to introduce the custom of saying the *Gloria*, which up to then had been recited or sung only by the bishops, as we have said, on Sundays and feasts of martyrs. On those days the bishops themselves said the *Ite, Missa est*, which was a sign of jurisdiction. The former custom became more widespread, and it also became a common practice for the priest to say the *Ite, Missa est*.

THE FIRST WORDS OF THIS HYMN ARE THOSE WITH which the angel saluted the shepherds on Christmas night: *Gloria in excelsis Deo.*

Everything in the stable spoke to the shepherds of heaven, but of an unclosed heaven, no longer merely a vague blue

---

[1] Cf. D. Cabrol O. S. B., *Le livre de la priére antique*, p. 153. This illustrious writer does not accept the opinion which attributes the *Gloria in excelsis* to St. Hilaire (fourth century). He says that if the holy bishop were the author of that hymn he would certainly have made a more explicit profession of faith in the consubstantially of the Word.

[2] *Idem*, p. 145.

sky which they were used to seeing above them, stretching away into the horizon.

Yes, everything spoke to them: the manger, the cold, the almost complete nakedness of the Child... his very appearance... he was so small!

And surely the more they contemplated him the more he reminded them of their little lambs, all so meek and gentle... And perhaps they thought how sweet it would be to hold that tiny Child in their arms; perhaps they dreamed of having in their flock a little lamb so beautiful and so good that he made them want to let themselves be shepherd by him...

These simple men were overwhelmed with enthusiasm and excitement. They felt they had to sing of such a sublime mystery. And, then, enlightened by the Light of the world, doubtless they realized that they should glorify that great mystery not only through the music of their rustic flutes, but also in their hearts.

We must be like them: a living testimony to God's glory.

Of what use are all our acts of piety, if we do not amend our life, if we do not fulfill our professional duties?

There are so many who sing the glories of the Lord, while they are covered in impurity.

There are many who proclaim them, clothed in vanity.

There are many who speak of them, while their heart is full of bitterness towards their neighbor. But you and I must not act thus.

THIS HYMN IS A PARAPHRASE OF THE *GLORIA PATRI*[3] and, at the same time, a continuation of the humble petitions of the *Kyrie*. The soul acknowledges, on the one hand, its weakness and its nothingness; and, on the other hand, it excites itself to admiration and joy at the sight of the majesty of God, and his omnipotence.

---

3   That is why it is called the 'greater doxology' as distinct from the *Gloria Patri* which is the 'lesser.' Doxology means glorification.

The soul then delights in glorifying God, in blessing his infinite perfections, which are manifested to us by his handiwork, especially by the work of our redemption. Love is always willing to give praise, it never tires of proclaiming its admiration, of singing it in songs overflowing with joy. In this glorification of God we find happiness and our peace. For he is the Spouse of our soul, our Father, our Brother, our Everything.

We give thanks to God for his great glory, for that glory is, in a way, *ours*; because Christ conquered it for us through his infinite merits and because it is promised to us, and will be attained by us, if we keep on the right road, if we persevere in the truth, if we live a *living life*.

THIS GLORIFICATION OF GOD IS PUT INTO PRACTICE through our good will.

If we fulfill the divine law, if we carry out the duties of our state faithfully and lovingly, then we give glory to God in a very real way. Our acts will then be in accordance, in agreement, with our principles; our life will be in conformity with that most noble end for which we were created. And our conscience will be at peace. *Et in terra pax hominibus*.

The soul addresses itself first to God the Father almighty: *Deus Pater Omnipotens*.

Then it adores, praises and glorifies the Lord Jesus. It blesses and gives thanks to the Son of the living God, who, according to the will of the Father, and through the co-operation of the holy Ghost, willed to be conceived in the most chaste womb of Virgin Mary and, with an incomprehensible love, willed to be, and is, our Lord: *Domine, Deus*.

The soul praises and blesses the Son of God: *Filius Patris*, because he became a lamb: *Agnus Dei*. He himself, the good Shepherd, became a lamb in order to save all men, by his death, death on a cross.

And this stainless Lamb did not hesitate to become the 'man of sorrows; and to burden himself with our sins, in order to take away the sins of the world, in order to reconcile man to God.

He had compassion on our infirmities; he loved us to the point of madness: he died for us on a cross, as if he forgot that he has a seat, in heaven, at the right hand of the Father: *qui sedes ad dexteram Patris.*

What greater proof of his love could he give us? 'Greater love than this no man hath, that a man lay down his life for his friends.'

Now, if he is such a friend of ours, why should we not ask him humbly to have pity on us: *miserere nobis*?

And he will indeed have mercy on us, we can be certain of that; he will listen to our requests, because he himself said: 'ask and you shall receive.'

But how are we to ask him in such a way that he may hear us?—*Suscipe deprecationem nostram.*

We must ask him humbly, confidently and with perseverance. Furthermore: so that he may hear our prayers, we must ask him to inspire us to pray for those things which he wishes to give us.[4] And in case he considers that he should not grant us our request, let us make an act of resignation to his will, or better still, an act of perfect acceptance. Let us say with all our heart: 'Not my will, but thine, O Lord, be done.'

'GOD ALONE IS HOLY BY ESSENCE, OR RATHER, HE is holiness itself.'[5] The sanctity of creatures is only a participation in God's holiness.

Holiness, when applied to God, means that most perfect love and unmovable fidelity with which he loves himself infinitely.

Tu solus sanctus...Jesu Christe...

'Thou only art holy, O Jesus Christ.' Only you are holy, because only you, through the Incarnation, are truly the Son

---

4   cf. Collect of the ninth Sunday after Pentecost.
5   D. Columba Marmion: *Christ the Life of the Soul*, I, 2.

of God; because you possess sanctifying grace in its fullness, sharing it with no one; because your soul was infinitely docile to the impulse of the Spirit of love, who inspired and governed all your movements, all your actions, and made them pleasing to your Father. Only you are holy, because you possess the divine life in its fullness. Only you are holy, because we hope for our holiness only from you.

The grace of pardon and all the graces of salvation, all the riches, all the supernatural benefits which abound in the world of souls, all come to us from you alone.

Therefore, may all our praise be given to you, O Jesus Christ. And, through you, may all our praise ascend to your Father for the unspeakable gift which he makes to us of you!

'Thou only art holy. Thou only art the Lord. Thou only, O Jesus Christ, art most high, with the Holy Ghost, in the glory of God the Father.' *Tu solus sanctus, tu solus Dominus, tu solus altissimus, Jesu Christe, cum Sancto Spiritu in gloria Dei Patris. Amen.*

V

Good News

THE BOOK OF THE GOSPELS WAS FORMERLY AN object of great religious worship. In the year 406 Saint Jerome wrote the following from Bethlehem: 'In all the churches of the east when reading the gospel candles are lighted, not to dispel the darkness, for the sun is already shining in the sky, but as a sign of joy.'[1]

A well-known Gallician pilgrim of the fourth century,[2] tells us that incense was burned during the reading of the gospel.

Saint Germain also[3] describes the rites which accompanied the reading of the gospel in the Gallic Mass:

'On reaching the holy gospel the procession came out, as if it represented the power of Christ to triumph over death, accompanied by beautiful choral harmonies and with seven candlesticks lighting, which represented the seven gifts of the holy Ghost...

'And then the deacon went up to the pulpit, or tribunal, which represented the throne of Christ in heaven, and chanted there the gifts of life, after which the clerics exclaimed: *Gloria tibi, Domine*, "glory be to thee, O Lord".'

In the sixteenth century more or less the same procession was formed. But it is interesting to note that, after the deacon had turned towards the north (ordo II) and read the gospel, the book was handed to a subdeacon in the procession who took it to be kissed by everyone between the pulpit and the apse.

FORMERLY ALSO THE GOSPEL BOOK WAS WRAPPED in precious cloths, and placed in a casket adorned with pure gold and precious stones. And who has not seen those beautiful

---

1 Quoted in the *Dictionnaire d'archéologie chrétienne et liturgie*, V, I, 777.
2 Etheria: *Peregrinatio ad loca sacra*.
3 *Dict. d'archéologie chrétienne et liturgie*, V, I, 777.

marginal miniatures in the manuscripts of the gospel, made by the pupils at the school of the well-known abbey of St. Gall and others? In our own day, in sung Masses with ministers, we still find a trace of that symbolic procession which formerly went to the place where the gospel was to be read or sung.

Let us see: the deacon takes the missal, goes and places it on the altar, and kneeling down, asks the Lord, in a beautiful prayer,[4] to purify his heart and his lips that he may announce the holy gospel in a worthy manner. Then he asks the celebrant for a blessing, and he gives it to him with these words: 'May the Lord be in thy heart and on thy lips, that thou mayst meetly and fitly announce his gospel.'

Then the procession begins: the thurifer goes first carrying the thurible, and at his side the master of ceremonies, with his hands joined; then the candle-bearers with their candles, lighting[5] symbols of our faith which makes us look on the word of Jesus as a light that we must follow; then the subdeacon, with his hands joined, and beside him the deacon carrying the missal. They all go to the place where the gospel is to be sung. All present rise to their feet.[6] On arriving there, the deacon chants the introduction to the reading of the gospel, which itself is a sacramental; he makes the sign of the Cross on it, at the beginning of the text, and then on himself: on his forehead, mouth and breast; he incenses the missal and goes on to sing the gospel of the day. Then the subdeacon allows the celebrant to kiss the book, and he says: 'By the words of the gospel may our sins be blotted out.' In fact, 'the hearing of the holy Gospel can produce this grace, for it has the virtue of awakening in the soul dispositions such as obtain pardon for sin.'[7]

---

4 'Cleanse my heart and my lips, O almighty God, who didst cleanse the lips of the prophet Isaias with a burning coal: vouchsafe through thy gracious mercy so to cleanse me that I may worthily proclaim thy gospel. Through Christ our Lord. Amen.'
5 In sung Masses for the dead the procession takes place without candles.
6 'With respect and fear,' St. Benedict says.
7 D. Vandeur: *The Holy Mass*, London 1928, p. 66

ALL OF THIS, MY FRIEND, REMINDS US OF THE respect and veneration we owe to the words of the gospel—which are the words of God himself—and to the missal in which they are written: the only liturgical book which is kissed and incensed, and on which the sign of the Cross is made. The gospel should be read and meditated many, many times. We should even memorise, not all perhaps, but at least the most notable passages. Priests should know it like the palm of their hand, and then they would never lack something to say in their sermons and in their work.

Saint Gregory the Great, in his *Pastoral Care*, says that every pastor has an undeniable duty to read and study the word of God with the greatest care and attention. While he was pope, sacred scripture was not only a manual of dogmatic and moral theology for the clergy, but also a book of meditation.

Does our conscience, perhaps, accuse us of being less zealous on this point — much less, usually — than many, many poor sinners?

'BLESSED ARE THEY THAT HEAR THE WORD OF GOD and keep it.'

On hearing the words of the gospel our heart should keep itself prepared, alert, open and docile. Let us, with Samuel, say to the Lord: 'Speak, Lord, for thy servant heareth.'

Prepared for everything?...We stand up when reading the gospel, in the attitude of one who is prepared to suffer everything for the sake of those sacred words...

Prepared to die?—If necessary, yes!

Prepared to die to ourselves, to our disorderly inclinations, to our own will? Yes. And this *is* necessary: every day, every moment of every day...

That is how you must be, my friend; and without the slightest delay or hesitation.

That is how you must be: not in the least halfhearted, without the slightest complaint.

That is how you must be...doing everything, giving everything, giving yourself, with your heart generously opened wide, manfully and *cheerfully*: bread given grudgingly never tastes very well to the poor...The apostle said: 'It is the cheerful giver God loves.'

YOU WILL ASK: EVERYTHING, LORD? THIS, YES, I will sacrifice to you. But that other thing Lord...it is so hard...

Can the Lord, who is so good, ask me to sacrifice this desire, this legitimate desire, this holy affection?

Could he not ask me to make other sacrifices, perhaps greater ones than this?

Ah! my friend, fix your eyes on the Crucifix and listen to what I have to say to you: Everything, everything...your most legitimate desires, your most holy ambitions, those occupations of yours which you carry out with the highest supernatural motives. Look: the best thing for you is to do *that thing* which he asks of you, in the *way* he asks it, in the *place* he asks it. Give him *that*...without hesitation.

A generous heart does not begin to weigh up or measure the arguments for and against what God asks. It is ready, always ready. At times it hurts, stings, draws blood...It is very hard, I know it is very hard. What matter?—The soul is faithful and knows that what God wants is always the best for us.

Your poor soul is confused? No wonder.

There will certainly be voices coming from inside and outside, suggesting, insinuating very quietly and cleverly that God has abandoned you. The soul hears these voices and, from time to time, trembles...but all this passes. It comes in waves, it goes in waves...and all, one after another, die away in soft foam...but the rock...stands firm.

In the faithful soul that is how peace reigns.

It is troubled, true, but not in its most noble and most delicate corner, for there it is united, firmly and invincibly, to the will of the Lord. It wants only what he wants, where he wants it, how he wants it, and, very often, only *because* he wants it. In these cases it feels no sensible consolation; but it is consoled—greatly consoled—by knowing that the Lord wants that soul to be where it is. And there it stays, through thick and thin...What else matters? The soul knows that he who is Everything is happy.

And you, my friend, how do you act?

GOOD NEWS! BUT WHAT IS THIS NEWS, ANNOUNCED and received with so much joy, like the fulfilment of some marvelous and extraordinary promise?

It is a 'new commandment': it is love!

Is it love for our friends, for our fellow-countrymen, tolerance of strangers and perhaps, in rare circumstances, of enemies? Is it love of others in return for their love, for our own good?

Ah, no! It is love of our brothers and friends; it is love of our enemies for the love of God. It is love of suffering, love of persecutions, for the sake of justice, for the love of God. It means forgetting ourselves in order to help others, for their good, with our eyes and heart fixed on God. It means dying to ourselves in order to *live* in God, so that God may *live* in us.

It is the Word becoming flesh and dwelling among us; becoming flesh in order to show us the way, *to be* the Way. It is Jesus, the Man-God, searching among the thorns for the lost sheep in order to lift it up on his shoulders and bring it back to the fold.

It is Jesus himself—O marvelous transaction!—in the Eucharist.

It is Saint Paul, willing to be doomed to separation from Christ for love of his spiritual sons, willing to be excommunicated for his persecutors (Rom. IX, 3).

It is Saint Stephen asking pardon, on his knees, for those who were barbarously stoning him to death.

It is Saint Peter of Verona, giving himself as ransom for slaves.

It is Saint John of God, throwing himself into flames in order to save the patients in the hospital he had founded.

It is Saint Teresa of Avila, wanting to die or to suffer.

It is Saint Mary Magdalen of Pazzi, wishing to suffer, to suffer and not to die.

It is Saint Gertrude the Great, of whom the Lord said: 'You will find me in the Tabernacle and in the heart of Gertrude.'

It is the religious, who offers himself as a total sacrifice, a living host which 'on being raised up, raised the whole world.'

It is the poor, the ill, those who suffer to 'fill up those things that are wanting of the sufferings of Christ' (Col. I, 24) and in this way prolong them.

It is the Communion of saints.

It is those souls who plunge themselves into God, so that in his bosom they may live with his life, which is 'living life.'

YOU ALSO, MY FRIEND, WHOEVER YOU MAY BE, HAVE an obligation to preach the good news.

It is true that not all are called to preach in the pulpit. As Saint Paul says, the Lord wants some of us to be apostles, others evangelists, others doctors... But if all are not called to preach in the pulpit, no one whatever his position or state in life, is dispensed from preaching by his example. And that is preaching *par excellence*; the most convincing way of preaching there is.

THE GOSPEL SHOULD BE THE LIGHT WHICH GUIDES our steps through all the paths of life: 'Thy word is a lamp to my feet' (Ps. 118, 105).

That path of light is the only one we must follow. All the rest are darkness and the shadow of death.

There are bound to be stones in the way, and tremendous precipices on all sides. But a soldier of God fears nothing, never looks back: he advances gracefully, straight ahead, his eyes fixed on heaven, fixed on his Lord, watching his least movements, anticipating his least desires.

It is the faithful soul, which the angels take by the hand lest he dash his foot against a stone in the way. My friend, let this faithful soul be you!

VI
A Host for a Host

MY FRIEND, HAVE YOU EVER NOTICED THAT HOST, that little host lying on the paten, which the priest raises on high as if offering it up?

That host, as white as snow, will very soon be transformed into the body and blood of your Lord.

It was he who willed and decided that it should be so.

If only you also were willing and decided to be a host![1] Perhaps you were sitting quietly among the shadows of death, when you should have been advancing rapidly along the path of light? Become now a host, in expiation for your sins. Love your brothers as yourself, for the love of God. Sacrifice yourself for them. Stop thinking only of yourself. Think very much about their needs. You must do that: you are a member of the mystical body of Christ. And there are so many ill and suffering members who need, perhaps not your sacrifices, but at least your prayers.[2]

Do not refuse them.

---

1 'The Offertory, in which nowadays only the celebrant and the ministers take part, is one of the most important rites to provide the faithful with a theological notion of the Eucharist.

'The Eucharist is not only the Communion of the consecrated host exposed for the veneration of the faithful; the Sacrifice is composed of two elements, one specific: the immolation or sacrifice, and the other generic: the oblation or offering.

'...The faithful, then must, through the mediation of the sacerdotal hierarchy, offer Jesus Christ and also offer themselves in the Mass. This spiritual oblation of themselves is manifested visibly by the offering of the material gifts which they contribute for the celebration of the Sacrifice, the sustenance of the cult and its ministers. Through this offering the faithful take an active and, so to speak, material part on the Offertory of the Mass.' Antonio Coelho, *Curso de Liturgia Romana*, Vol. 2, no. 135.

2 Let us often think, with D. Marmion: 'I can do much for the interests of souls redeemed by the blood of this Son; without my prayer, which is that of thy Son, there might perhaps be some at this moment who would be lost for eternity.' *Christ, the Ideal of the Monk*, London 1926, p. 332.

Do you think your prayers are worth nothing? It is true that they may be useless in themselves, in as much as they come from you, but they certainly become very valuable through the infinite value of the merits of Christ, who is the head of the mystical body to which you belong. Never forget the interests of Jesus: that little expression contains everything.

ARE YOU READY TO OPEN YOUR HEART EVEN MORE? Come on, offer yourself as a host of praise and adoration. Have you ever stopped to examine your inclinations, your talents, your strength? Have you ever tried, by all the means at your disposal, to find out what the Lord wants of *you*? Perhaps—it may be—he wants you to detach yourself, not only *affectively*, which is the duty of everyone, but also *effectively*, from the things of this world? Have you thought seriously about that? Remember that it is the most important duty of your life! Have you consulted a devout, prudent and practical priest on the matter? Have you consulted, above all, Jesus himself? Go now and speak to him. Open your heart to him, wide, with great simplicity. Ask him to show you what his will is, insist, persist until you get an answer.

He will not fail to show you what he wants of you. And if you see that his will points in that direction, then you must go in that direction. Start now! You will find plenty of thorns in the path ... but, remember this: you will also have, always, his help, his grace; at times you will even feel some little signs of his attention, coming to you from heaven.

BE A HOST!
Are you willing to place yourself also, generously, on the paten?

But look: once you decide to do it, never reverse your decision ... Not even so much as a backward glance. Do not take back from the Lord the least part of anything you give him.

No, do not take back anything. Because, believe me, to do that would be to rob the Lord; every offering you make is a holy thing. But if you have offered *yourself*, consecrated yourself...!

Perhaps he asks no more of you than the little things of every day, which, by their monotony, are also rather hard. But perhaps he asks more, perhaps he asks the sacrifice of your most legitimate desires, of everything, absolutely everything.

Do you want to go even further?

The way is narrow, I know, but there is so much light...

Do all the little actions of each day for love of him. If you are not clearly and expressly called to extraordinary things — well then, try to do what you have to do better and better, your everyday tasks, in whatever circumstances you may be. That is what God wants you to do: that is his will. I know you find it hard, perhaps very hard. But that, believe me, is what gives value and merit to your actions. Do not deceive yourself. Sanctity, being a saint, consists precisely in that: in doing *for love* the little tasks we have to do every day.

Do you think that in different circumstances you could be more holy? Perhaps... but that other situation does not exist now. And reality is what matters.

You are not in that new situation now, and perhaps you will never be. You imagination dreams of those things, and your imagination is mad. But at least let that highest and most noble part of your will contradict it and decide to sanctify yourself where you really are. You can be certain of one thing: your cross will follow you wherever you go.

IN TIME OF SICKNESS DO NOT SAY: 'LOOK AT ALL my works of piety to which I was so devoted, and now here I am unable to do anything, at times I cannot even say an *Our Father*.'

No, do not say: 'I cannot do anything.' You cannot, it is true, do things you *would like* to do, but you can do that extraordinarily great thing: the will of God. You are there because he wants you to be there.

You know all these things, you are convinced that they are all true. Still, you are not completely convinced, but only in a theoretical way. Your heart is not sufficiently detached from things, it is not on the alert.

Little birds hop lightly on the ground; but at the least noise they are ready to take flight. You must be the same. Your soul, too, must be ready to soar on high the moment it hears any sound of divine movement.

ARE YOU NOW IN SOME BRILLIANT POSITION, besieged by all the glories of publicity, in spite of the fact that your modesty would like you to be well hidden under a bushel?

If you have been placed in that position, not through your own pride, however well disguised, but by the express will of the Lord,[3] then be quiet and suffer with great patience all the publicity, exaggerated praise, misunderstandings of all kinds, enmities, envy, intrigues, calumnies: in short, everything.

And if, suddenly, you are reduced to obscurity and silence, continue to be content. If in that obscurity you are mortified by all the monotony of the most humble actions of each day, then rejoice even more.

Be joyful always. The Lord will never fail you, in any situation, under any circumstances; he is always ready to enlighten you, to strengthen you, to be more and more closely united to you.

---

3   Let us see how St. Anselm reconciles humility with obedience in relation to the acceptance and retention of offices and honours: Not only should we give no sign of great pleasure, neither saying nor doing anything which might encourage others to bestow honour on us, but we should try to flee from it by every possible means, except sin. However, those on the other side of the affair, who have the authority, should, of course, 'oblige' the person in question, if he is the most worthy, to accept the task. Then the person chosen should accept only out of fear of God and obedience, and his conscience can be at peace before God. Cf. *Lettres spirituelles choisies*, XXXIV and others.

ADVANCE! YOU SEE: THE LORD IS CALLING YOU! DO you not feel the delights of his presence?[4] Good! They will encourage you. But be careful... Some day you may have to do without them. Be on the alert. Do not and in that way you will share in the holiness of him who became a host, a victim for us.

A HOST FOR A HOST!

'The prayers with which the Church accompanies this divine Sacrifice make it clearly understood that this oblation also belongs to those who assist at it. What does the priest say, after the Offertory, when he turns a second time towards the people before singing the Preface? "Brethren, pray that *my* sacrifice *and yours* may be acceptable to God the Father almighty." Again, in the prayer preceding the Consecration, the priest beseeches God to be mindful of the faithful who are present, those, he says, "for whom we offer, or who offer up to thee this sacrifice of praise for themselves and those belonging to them." And then, extending his hands over the oblation, he asks God to accept it as the oblation of His whole spiritual family gathered around the altar: *Hanc igitur*. As you see, it is the faithful united to the priest and, through him, to Jesus Christ, who offer this sacrifice. Christ is the supreme and principal pontiff; the priest is his minister chosen by him; lastly the faithful,

---

4 'We must not confuse this devotion with certain of its effects. It does not consist in feelings or sensible consolation; however frequent these may be, they are accidental nonetheless, depending as much on temperament and circumstances as on our Lord. It is good to feel sweetness in God's service. The inspired singer says: *Gustate et videte quoniam suavis est Dominus*, "Taste and see that the Lord is sweet" (Ps. XXXIII, 9), but this does not constitute the essence of devotion... it encourages us and stimulates love.

'Devotion is the consecration of our whole self to God; it is the most delicate flower and the purest fruit of love, for it is love giving itself wholly to the beloved being. It is this totality in love which is the mark of devotion. When we love with all our heart, we do not count the cost, we willingly spend ourselves without measure for the sake of those we thus love.' D. Marmion: *Christ, the Ideal of the Monk*, London 1926, p.332.

in their rank, participate in the sacred priesthood and in all the acts of Christ.'⁵

A HOST FOR A HOST!

Yes. It is not Christ alone who offers himself; it is the mystical Christ, the Christ *in us*. Furthermore, the sacrifice is offered by all the faithful and not only by the priests. What the latter do especially, by virtue of their ministry, is done by the universal offering of the faithful.⁶

AT THE MOMENT OF THE OFFERTORY THE PRIEST pours a little water into the chalice, which already contains the wine, and says this beautiful prayer: 'O God, who in a wonderful manner didst create and ennoble human nature, and still more wonderfully renewed it; grant that by the mystery of this water and wine, we may be made partakers of our humanity, Jesus Christ thy Son, our Lord: who liveth and reigneth with thee in the unity of the Holy Ghost, one God, world without end.'

The priest then offers the chalice, praying that it may be acceptable to God *'with an odour of sweetness.'*

This mystery of the mingling of water with wine is, in the first place, the wonderful union of humanity with the divinity in Jesus Christ. It is also the union of Christ with his Church, his mystical body. We are the water.

'The water symbolises the Christian people. That is why we are forbidden, in consecrating the chalice, to offer either wine alone or water alone. To offer the consecrated wine without mixing water with it would seem to imply that Christ can be offered without us; therefore only when the wine and the water are mixed and united is the whole of the spiritual and celestial sacrament fulfilled.'⁷

---

5   D. Columba Marmion: *Christ the Life of the Soul*, p. 254.
6   Cf. Innocent III: *De sacro altaris mysterio*, L. III C 5.
7   St. Cyprian: Letter LXIII.

A HOST FOR A HOST!

Let us become a host, a victim, with Jesus.

Let us offer him some sacrifices, not in any abstract way, but very concretely: *this* and *that*.

For instance: let us offer him the affliction caused us by some pleasure which our inclinations desire, but which is forbidden by the law of God.

Do you want more sacrifices? It is so easy to find them everywhere, at every moment! Get up early and overcome your laziness; spend the day working and avoid idleness and negligence; at table we can sacrifice the dainties; when engaged in a conversation we can sacrifice the desire to say or listen to many useless things. We can sacrifice our eyes, deciding not to look at attractive things which our curiosity entices us to see. We can restrain our tongue from singing our own praises, from speaking about ourselves, from publicising the defects of others.

Let us offer to the Lord in advance all those natural graces which the years and illness may bring us from time to time. Let us sacrifice to the Being who is eternal our own poor being which perishes so quickly; let us act so that our mortal life, with its sacrifices, may be a continual homage to his immortality.

A host for a host!

Let us be victims in union with that most holy Victim. Let us be ready to give everything to God, to suffer everything, to accept everything, for love of him. Let us be deeply penetrated with the sentiments of Christ; let us unite ourselves to those sentiments in an intense love for the eternal Father, for our brothers, for the salvation of souls, in complete abandonment to the most holy will of God, especially in those things which our nature finds most difficult.

Lord, with your Church we often pray thus: 'That we may be hosts worthy to be offered eternally to you.'

WE ARE VERY WILLING TO SACRIFICE OURSELVES...

until it comes to the moment of doing so. Illness prostrates us. With the grace of God let us accept it cheerfully, deep down in our heart, even if, as is natural, we find it difficult.

Then come moments of fervour; we are thrilled by the idea of suffering for our brothers in the Lord, of suffering 'to fill up those things that are wanting of the sufferings of Christ.' And at times we even think that it would be quite easy to give our life itself as a holocaust, an offering, for this lofty end. But if the hand of God presses a little heavier on us then discouragement comes, like a cloud in a blue sky, covering over the horizon...

And if he leaves us, if he hides from us... then all our illusions disappear, all our great hopes vanish, like the swallows in autumn. Then we feel completely alone, in close contact with our weakness, recognising our great misery; and this contact and this recognition are very painful to our self-esteem, but very good for our soul, because the more clearly we see that we are nothing, the more we see how much we are in need of him, who is everything.

Is it not true that in moments of sensible fervour, of spiritual consolation, we often say: Lord, whatever you want... Thy will be done...? Because in those moments it happens that his coincides with ours.

But if he wants us to do something which our nature finds hard, if he asks us to make difficult sacrifices... then we think that the Lord has changed... what we really loved was not the will of the Lord, pure and simple, but our own... How often he permits these cold, dry periods and these lapses so that we may feel what we are and acknowledge what we are not.

VII

Actio I: The Preface

THE WORD *ACTIO* IS A CONTRACTION OF *SACRUM agere, operare, facere*, all expressions with which the ancients designated sacrifice. Therefore sacrifice consists essentially in an immolation, in the destruction of some sacrificial victim.

The oblation, or offering, is only an essential preparation, just as the Communion is its necessary complement. That is why, in primitive language, the term sacrifice, or *action*, is reserved for the immolation.

In the Mass, it is true, there is no real immolation; there is an unbloody renewal of the bloody immolation of the Cross, a mystical immolation, intentional, equivalent, or, in short, a real *oblation* of the Victim previously *immolated* on Calvary; and that renewal takes place in the double Consecration. But the Consecration is surrounded by a series of rites, which constitute with it one single unity, a single action. This action lasts from the *Dominus vobiscum* after the Secret to the *Amen* before the *Pater Noster*. Originally it was one single prayer of thanksgiving—*Eucaristia*—which sang of God's blessing from the creation to the descent of the holy Ghost and the admission of the faithful into everlasting glory. Nowadays the thread of ideas is broken by the *Sanctus* which divides the *Action* into two unequal parts: the first, recited aloud, the Preface, the second, recited silently, the Canon.[1]

THE WORD *PREFACE* IS COMMONLY TAKEN NOWAdays to mean an introduction to the Canon. Formerly it was part of the Canon. It is one of the most important prayers in the Liturgy, because of its antiquity, because of its structure and because of the ideas it expresses.

It is the eucharistic prayer, the supreme act of thanksgiving.

---

1 Cf. Coelho: *Curso de Liturgia Romana*, II, p. 172.

HAVING SALUTED THE FAITHFUL WITH THAT BEAUtiful salutation *Dominus vobiscum,* the Lord be with you, the celebrant bids them raise their hearts on high: *sursum corda.* Why is this? So that, free of all earthly cares, of all perverse or vain thoughts, they may give thanks to God our Lord with great dignity, attention and devotion. And to that call to attention, the faithful reply—if only they were speaking the truth!—*habemus ad Dominum*: we have raised up our hearts to the Lord.

It is the ideal moment to persuade them to give thanks to God: *Gratias agamus Domino Deo nostro.* And when he says these words the priest raises his eyes to heaven and joins his hands, thus expressing the forcefulness and sincerity of his sentiments.

Then the faithful remember the Lord's great gifts and his goodness:

It was he who deigned to create man in his own image and likeness.

It was he who, seeing man separated from God, after the fall, did not hesitate to give his only begotten Son who, in turn, deigned to become a man and died for love of men.

It was he...what more must I say? It was he who gave their souls so many and such wonderful graces.

Then the faithful feel the need of telling the Lord, and repeating to him many times, how thankful they are; they feel they must confess solemnly that it is *meet and just* that he should be thanked, very often...

And that is why the priest goes on to say, in the name of all, that 'it is truly meet and just, right and availing unto salvation, that we should at all times and in all places give thanks to thee,' in prosperity and in adversity, in times of fervour and in times of great sterility: always.

But do not merely say it with your lips! Confirm it, translate it into deeds, when the opportunity arises.

We are very far from that conformity, that equality, which should exist between what we say and what we do, what we appear to be and what we are! Indeed, how little truth there is in our lives. If men knew what we are *in reality*!... But God knows, for his eyes are always resting on the good and on the bad: penetrating eyes, terrible, yes... But paternal and loving eyes. My friend, let us remember this, very often.

AND LET US NEVER FORGET—FOR THIS FUNDAMENtal—that it is through Jesus Christ that we must thank God, for no act of thanksgiving is more worthy of our Father-God than that which ascends into heaven through his Son, Jesus Christ. He is the Way, the only way, that will take us to heaven.

How many souls there are who, in practice, are ignorant of this basic principle, who get lost in little details, and make an *end* of what is only a *means*: and make an obstacle of what was meant to be a help!

It is *through Christ* that the majesty of God is praised and adored by the angels and archangels, by the powers and dominations, by the heavens, the heavenly hosts and all the blessed Seraphim.

And thus—how beautiful is the Communion of Saints!—we all ask the Lord, through the mouth of the celebrant, to allow us to join our own supplicatory voices with those innumerable hosts in awe, wonderment and great enthusiasm, in order to sing with them *una voce*, with one voice, that hymn of victory in praise of the blessed Trinity which Isaias (VI, 3) heard the Seraphim sing beside the throne. And we follow it with the acclamations which resounded in Jerusalem on palm Sunday:

'Holy, holy, holy, Lord God of hosts!

'Heaven and earth are full of thy glory. Hosanna in the highest. Blessed is he that cometh in the name of the Lord. Hosanna in the highest.'

How overwhelming is the Preface!

While it is being recited or sung, we can think of nothing but Jesus Christ in the presence of his heavenly Father, in all his majesty, supreme Head of the whole Church, triumphant, suffering and militant, through which resounds this majestic song of his praise.

And when all present, all those assisting at Mass, sing with one voice (when will this custom be introduced among us?) it reminds one of heaven itself, where all the heavenly armies sing and repeat, without ceasing, these same words of praise and adoration!

In truth, the prayer of the Church is a heavenly prayer.

If we meditated deeply on these most beautiful prayers, and tried to translate our enthusiasm into works, works which conform with what we say, then the fruit of assisting at Mass would be completely different: individuals would be different, families would be different, society itself would be different.

And yet we are unwilling to believe in that! We agree that it is quite true... but we do no more. Perhaps we desire that it should be so, that it should become more and more so, but we do not desire it *effectively*, we do not put our desire into practice, we stop short at a vague hope... Good, my friend: right now, with great generosity, resolve firmly to make of the Eucharist—a sacrifice and a sacrament—the centre of your interior life: and to try to act always, as far as possible, in agreement with the words which you pronounce, together with the celebrant and the rest of the faithful. Begin today, right now. Do not let all that light from on high be lost.

VIII

Actio II: The Canon

THE SECOND PART OF THE *ACTIO* IS COMMONLY known as the *Canon,* that is the rule or mode of celebrating the Sacrifice.

At the beginning of the seventh century it already had the same form as it has today. Originally it began at the *Sursum Corda.* Today it begins immediately after the last *Hosanna* of the *Sanctus.* It is separated from the Preface by the *Sanctus.* The two words *Te igitur* of the prayer which comes after the *Sanctus,* try, in a way, to link up the broken thread, because the whole *Actio,* which lasts from the *Dominus vobiscum* before the Preface up to and including the *Per ipsum,* is one unit. The erroneous idea that the Preface was distinct from the prayers following it was encouraged by the increase in size which the illumination of the letter T of the *Te igitur* began to get, so that little by little it came to occupy a whole page on its own.

During the *Canon* nowadays there is usually complete silence. Let us also be silent; let us impose silence on all our cares and distractions and let us follow the priest with profound respect. The most majestic Mystery of the altar is going to be celebrated.

IN THE FIRST PART OF THE *TE IGITUR* THE CELEbrant asks God to condescend to bless our offerings. In the second part, which begins with the word *In primis,* he prays for the necessities of the holy Church. He asks him to grant it peace—a grace which includes all the others—to protect, unite and govern it throughout the world; he asks him to guide the holy Father, Christ's vicar on earth, father of God's great family, and to direct his bishop, who is for him a sacred bond of unity. Finally, he prays for all true sons of the Catholic and Apostolic Church. It is *in union with all of those* that he celebrates the holy Sacrifice.

'On the point of accomplishing the most solemn act of religion, the assembly feels the need of openly affirming its community in faith and charity with those who have gone before, and are now still united to them in Christ. Across time and space it takes by the hand the Apostles and the Martyrs, all those who profess the same orthodox Faith, so as to join them, in a manner, with the act which it is going to renew after them and with them.'[1]

Let us never forget that the eucharistic Sacrifice is the sacrament of unity.

LET US NOT FORGET THAT THE GREAT DEVOTION of the Liturgy is to pray for the Church. It is also the devotion of many great souls, of those who give second place to their own petty everyday interests in order to care first of all for the holy Church, the immaculate Spouse of Jesus Christ, to see that it is beautiful like God himself, powerful in all its actions, victorious in its perpetual struggles.

Let us expand, let us increase our piety; let us be noble, lofty souls, who seek, above all things, the glory of God and of his Christ, and who seek it through the Church.

MEMENTO DOMINE...REMEMBER, O LORD, THY SERvants, men and women...This is the moment when the priest prays for the intentions of living individuals,[2]

---

1 D. Morin: *The Ideal of the Monastic Life*, London 1914, p. 95.
2 Since God gives special graces to those for whom the holy Sacrifice is celebrated, why should we not have Mass said for the conversion of sinners in general and of some sinner, in whom we are interested, in particular?

If we cannot get them to assist at the holy Sacrifice, we should try by other means to make them participate in the power of Christ's immolation to remit all sins. We shall achieve this result by having Masses offered for their intention. Many, very many, people who pray for the grace of conversion for some person they love forget that, in Christ's sacrifice, they have the remission of *all* sins. This does not mean that they should neglect acts of self-denial, mortification, prayer, practice of the virtues in union with Christ for that intention. It only means especially those for whom the Mass is being celebrated. This is the *special* fruit of the Mass. But there is another *more special* fruit which is always the property of the priest who celebrates.[3] What enormous fruit we can gain from the *Memento*! What a privilege it is to be present on the lips and in the thoughts of the priest just when he is going to accomplish the most tremendous and most sacred act that can be imagined! Ah! if only we had faith in that!

The priest then prays for all those present, those who are assisting at the Mass. Theology teaches us that they have a very special right[4] to the fruits of the holy Sacrifice: first—and more than any of the others—the ministers or the server, and then all the assembly.

Ah! if we always attended with real faith and devotion—*quorum tibi fides cognita est nota devotio*...[5]

He prays not only for those present, but also for their relatives and friends, present or absent: *pro se suisque omnibus.*

He prays for the redemption of their souls, the hope of their salvation and even for their bodily safety. *Et memoriam venerantes.* This is the commemoration of the Church triumphant.

Let us honour, says the celebrant, the memory of the blessed Virgin, mother of God, of the blessed apostles, of the holy martyrs and of all the saints.

---

that the offering of the Mass for the intention of sinners, is the best work of mercy which we can do for love of them. Cf. Abbé C. Grimaud: *Ma Messe*, p. 141.
3 Not because he *celebrates*, for in a way all the faithful are co-celebrants, but because he *officiates*, because he *consecrates*.
4 Anyone who assists at a parish Mass receives the same graces as he would get from a Mass celebrated for his own intention because, according to many venerable theologians, from a mass offered for many, each one receives the same fruits as he would receive if it were offered for him alone.
5 'This sacrifice does not act in us, like the sacraments, *ex opera operato*. Its fruits are inexhaustible, but they are in great part measured by our inward dispositions. In every Mass there are infinite possibilities for us of perfection and holiness; but the measure of the graces we receive is the measure of our faith and of our love. You will have noticed that when, before the Consecration, the priest enumerates those he wishes to recommend to God, he ends by speaking of all those present, but in indicating the dispositions of their hearts: *quorum tibi fides cognita est et nota devotio.*' D. Marmion: *Christ the Life of the Soul*, p. 254.

'The sacrifice is offered, not to the saints, but to God and God alone. It is offered only in *honour* and in *memory* of the saints. To commemorate them is, indirectly, to ask their intercession. To offer the holy Sacrifice in their honour is to give God thanks for his predilection of them; to obtain for ourselves the strength to imitate their lives and to practise the principal virtues for which they were distinguished, for they pray for us.'[6]

First comes our Lady, conceived without sin, God's mother and our mother, a virgin before and after her delivery.

Then come the apostles, those wonderful foundation stones of the great edifice which is the mystical body of Christ:

Peter is the rock on which Jesus Christ built his Church; the vicar of Christ on earth; the shepherd of the flock and the prince of the apostles; to him were entrusted the keys of the kingdom of heaven.

Let us imitate the faithful of the early Church who never ceased praying to God for him who, out of humility, wished to be crucified with his head down, but let us also pray very much for his successor, the present pope.[7] All Catholics have a serious duty to do so.

Paul, who had been a bitter enemy of the Lord's disciples, but who then became the Vessel of election, is the illustrious doctor of the gentiles, who was willing to be separated from the Lord and excommunicated in disgrace for love of his spiritual sons.

Andrew, who saluted the 'precious cross' and asked it to receive a disciple of him who died on it for love of us.[8]

---

6 D. Vandeur: *op. cit.* p. 198.
7 Prayer for the Pope (to be found in the missal): 'O God, the shepherd and ruler of all the faithful, look down favourably on thy servant N., whom thou hast been pleased to appoint pastor over thy Church, grant, we beseech thee, that he may benefit both by word and example those over whom he is set, and thus attain unto life eternal, together with the flock committed to his care. Through our Lord.'
8 Cf. Baring-Gould: *The Lives of the Saints,* Nov. 30.

Actio II: The Canon

James, the Greater, brother of Saint John who, with his brother and Peter, was chosen to be a witness of our Lord's Transfiguration and whose body is venerated at Compostela, in Spain.

John, the beloved disciple, the evangelist who soared on high like an eagle in magnificent flight when speaking of the Word made flesh.

Thomas, whose doubt obtained for us such certainty, who on touching his Master's flesh healed the wounds of our infirmity.

James, the Less, a cousin of the Lord and brother of the apostle Judas Thaddaeus, was thrown from the top of the temple... It was he who proclaimed that 'faith without good works is dead.'

Philip, who asked the Lord to show him the Father, and said that he would ask nothing more. And Christ answered him: 'Have I been so long a time with you and have you not known me? Philip, he that seeth me seeth the Father also.'

Bartholomew, who was flayed alive and then suspended on a Cross to die in agonies.

Matthew, who is represented by an animal with a human face, because he began his gospel with a list of the ancestors from whom Jesus, as man, was descended.

Simon the Chanaanite, who announced the gospel to the peoples of the east.

Thaddaeus (Judas) a cousin of Jesus who was martyred with Simon in Persia.

Then come the pope-martyrs:

Linus, who was Saint Peter's immediate successor in the government of the Church.

Cletus, the third pope, converted by Saint Peter.

Clement, author of a letter to the Corinthians, a valuable document dating from the first centuries of Christianity.

Sixtus, of whom Saint Cyprian says that 'he was a lover of peace and excellent in every kind of virtue.'

Cornelius, who opposed the first anti-pope Novation.

Then come other illustrious saints:

Cyprian, bishop of Carthage, 'whose works are more brilliant than the sun,' as Saint Jerome says.

Laurence, the first of the seven deacons at the service of the Roman church in the time of pope Sixtus. When his persecutor demanded the *treasures* of the Church, he showed him hundreds of poor people.

Chrysogonus, a Roman priest who helped Saint Anastasia in the holy work of comforting the Christians who were in prison or condemned to torture.

John and Paul, of noble family, who were horrified when they saw an idol; they exclaimed: 'Lord, remove that abominable object from before our eyes...,' and they were beheaded.

If only we had such a horror of sin, of all the idols of this world!

Cosmas and Damian, brothers, distinguished doctors, great and apostolic healers of bodies and souls.

WHAT A WONDERFUL LIST OF HOSTS, OF VICTIMS! With what great devotion we should pronounce their names!

And notice, as Dom Vandeur says, that the mere fact of being named in the Canon of the Mass, at this solemn and divine moment, gives the saints more honour and glory than any other pious practice.

LET US CONSIDER, MY FRIEND, HOW WONDERFUL it is to be able to repeat on the altar the very words with which so many priests, full of fervour and piety, have celebrated the holy Sacrifice for century after century!

These prayers of the Canon were established at the time of the martyrs, and in the funeral chapels of the catacombs.

How edifying and consoling is this thought!

AND NOW, MY FRIEND, WE HAVE COME TO THOSE most solemn prayers which precede the Consecration. At this moment the Church militant, the Church suffering and the Church triumphant all have, so to speak, their eyes fixed on the altar. A most solemn moment!

Let us intensify our interior recollection, my friend, and try to assist with less indifference at this great *Mystery of faith*.

IX
Actio III: The Consecration

HANC IGITUR.

The priest spreads his hands over the chalice and the host, as the high priest did formerly over the victim which was sacrificed in expiation for the sins of the people. Now Jesus, the only victim worthy of God, is sacrificed for us.

The priest asks the Lord graciously to accept this sacrifice offered for himself and for all God's sons, this 'oblation of our service,' as the sacred text says.

THEN COMES THE PRAYER *QUAM OBLATIONEM*, whose purpose is to obtain from God the grace of transubstantiation.

Not that it denies the power of the words of Consecration which, spoken by the priest in the name of Christ, produce the transubstantiation; but their purpose is to call on and proclaim the power of God the Sanctifier, which converts the substance of the bread and wine into the substance of Jesus' body and blood.

On finishing this prayer, a lively sentiment of tenderness, provoked by the words *dilectissimi Filii tui,* forces, as it were, the priest to join his hands as if to embrace and hold the beloved Son of the Father, our Lord Jesus Christ.

And here we have reached the most solemn moment of the holy Mass, the Consecration.

Qui pridie... 'This formula is the most venerable of all, not only because of its origin—it is almost all taken from the synoptics and Saint Paul,—or because of the object of its narration—the institution of the blessed Eucharist,—but also and especially because of its effect: it brings about the conversion of the substance of the bread and wine into the substance of the body and blood of Jesus, and reproduces in an unbloody way the bloody sacrifice of the supreme Pontiff of humanity.

'It is the central point around which all the formulas and ceremonies gravitate; it is the most majestic moment of the holy Mass. The priest, who up to this point acts in the name of Jesus Christ, as his minister, now disappears before the sacred person of Jesus himself who comes to repeat the gestures, words and miracles of the last supper, who comes to perform the supreme mystery of our faith, *mysterium fidei*, which in former times the deacon acclaimed and which even today the priest confesses in a fervent outburst of faith which obliges him to interrupt the formula of the consecration of the chalice. The celebrant exposes the consecrated host and chalice, raising them up for the adoration of the faithful.'[1] The faithful should raise their eyes to contemplate their God hidden under the sacramental appearance and afterwards should bow their head to adore him.

And the transubstantiation is accomplished.

'The simplicity with which we beg for the great miracle of transubstantiation,' says Father Chaignon,[2] 'is similar to that which makes holy Scripture so sublime when it records the power of God in the act of creation: "Be light made, and light was made" (Gen. 1, 3); and in the no less wonderful miracle of the incarnation of the Word in Mary's womb: "Be it done unto me according to thy word. And the Word was made flesh".'

SURELY THOSE WHO HAVE RECEIVED THE GRACE AND the honour of exercising such a sublime ministry should willingly remain in perpetual admiration, in a continual act of acknowledgement and love of our God, of Jesus Christ, our high Priest! Truly the priesthood is the greatest dignity on earth. 'O how great and honourable is the office of priests, to

---

1 Coelho: *op. cit.* o. 182.
2 *Le prêtre á l'autel*, Liège, 1871, p. 216.

whom is given power to consecrate with the holy words of consecration the Lord of all Majesty, to bless him with their lips, to hold him in their hands, to receive him into their mouths and to minister him to others! O how clean should be the hands, how pure the mouth, how holy the body and how undefiled the heart of a priest, into whom so often enters the Author of all cleanliness! Truly there ought to proceed from the mouth of a priest, who so often receives the sacrament of Christ's body, no word but what is holy, honest and useful.

'His eyes should be simple and chaste, that so often behold the body of Christ. His hands should be pure and lifted up to heaven, which so often touch the Creator of heaven and earth.'[3]

LET NO PRIEST EVER FORGET THAT 'TO CELEBRATE Mass, to execute the noble functions of that sacred ministry, without first of all seeking to some extent his own crucifixion, would be to accept the honours and refuse the sacrifices, to expose oneself to God's vengeance.'

'Jesus Christ is the great master of all souls, he nourishes them with his own flesh, with his own blood, with his whole being... And in the same way no one who receives the task of shepherding souls can shirk the duty of nourishing them with his whole self.'[4]

My friend, let us honour all priests. Do you know the story of that saintly young man ordained by Saint Francis de Sales? Well, this young man had the privilege of being able to see his guardian Angel, who walked with him always in visible form. Until he became a priest the Angel always walked in front. Then, when Saint Francis de Sales ordained him, the Angel refused to go before him, and made the new priest go first! So great in the eyes of the Angels is the dignity of the priesthood. There is a lesson which that Angel taught us, poor sinners.

---

3 *Imitation of Christ:* Book IV, XI.
4 D. Jean d' Hemptinne: *Une âme bénédictine, Pensée* LXXXV.

As for us, my friend, who receive the Lord into our hearts so often, perhaps every day, how clean we should be, how chaste, how pure! What will become of us if we do not receive him as well as we possibly can?

And then let us not forget that we are temples of God: how are we to give him to others if we do not know how to keep him in ourselves? If we do not pray, if we do not converse with him, how are we to know what he wants of us or what we have to do to please him?

So we see why there is so much effort lost, so much fruitless apostolate. And why? Because our soul is not in it.

LET US NOT WORRY ABOUT OURSELVES IN SUCH A way that we see nothing else, that we do not think of others. For he who truly loves God must love the souls which belong to God.[5] But neither must we give ourselves in a way that may be detrimental to our own spiritual life.[6] Because the fact is this: if we do not fill ourselves full of him first of all we will not be able to work fruitfully. For how can we give what we do not possess?

So, my friend, let us try first of all to fill ourselves with him and then we will be able to give to others the overflow of our interior life, of the divine sap which saturates our soul. But we cannot lose ourselves for the sake of saving others. And we would certainly be lost if we gave away that sap which we need ourselves; because then our interior life

---

5 'When the soul begins to love, it rises up and advances towards God; and when one loves more, one gives oneself to one's neighbor in whom one sees God, one imitates Jesus in his love of souls.' D. Pie d'Hemptinne: *Une âme bénédictine. Pensée,* XLI. 'Concerning love of our neighbor, I am convinced of one thing and it is that, in the interior life, the soul cannot withdraw itself from the world around it in order to love only Christ, hidden within self.' *Idem.*, Letter of the 7th October, 1901.

6 'Worry which acts to the detriment of recollection is evidence of a very unenlightened love. That is to prefer some occurrence to the peace of Christ, the only real good and source of everything good. So our activity must spring from recollection and get all its fertility from it, but without ever letting ourselves become completely absorbed.' *Ibid., Pensée,* IV.

would decrease and with it the possibility of giving life to others. We would be harming them also in this way.

UNDE ET MEMORES. 'AS OFTEN AS YOU SHALL DO THIS,' said the Lord, 'you shall do it in remembrance of me.' So the priest, in this prayer, as if fulfilling the Lord's wish, calls to mind the great mysteries of Jesus: his blessed passion, his resurrection and ascension into heaven. Then, in the prayer *Supra quae* 'the Church reminds God, with exquisite delicacy, of three sacrifices of the old Law which were pleasing to him, those of Abel, Abraham and Melchisedech, and asks him to deign to look favourably and benevolently on this offering as he was pleased by those sacrifices of the Old Law.'[7]

Here once again we see that it is not only Jesus who is offered, but Jesus and his mystical body.

THE PRIEST BOWS LOW—AN ACTION SUGGESTED BY the word *Supplices*—and says this prayer. It marks the approach of holy Communion, for it speaks of 'reception, by participation at this altar, of the most sacred body and blood of thy Son.'

'The Church asks that the oblation be carried by the hand of the Angel of the Lord to the altar on high, in the presence of the Divine Majesty; so that the earthly sacrifice may form but one with that of Heaven, and produce in our souls the same effects of grace.'[8]

Always the idea of *unity*...

---

7   If Christ alone were the Victim without his mystical Body, he would not have to beg the favour of being carried by the angels to God; for he is King of the heavenly court, and sits at the right of his Father.
Besides the one spotless Host, there are other hosts not quite so pure. That is why the Church asks God to inspire in her children the same dispositions as the holy patriarchs had.
This insistence in the liturgy that we must ask God to look favourably on our offering is also an invitation to us to work very hard in order to become more and more pleasing to his infinite Majesty. Cf. Grimaud: *Ma Messe*, p. 71.
8   D. Morin: *op. cit.* p. 96.

AND NOW COMES THE *MEMENTO* OF THE DEAD, another interruption in the Canon. The priest commemorates those who died in the true faith, for whom the Mass is being offered, and prays that they and all those who sleep in the Lord, may be granted 'a place of refreshment, light and peace.' These are the souls in purgatory. Saint Jerome says that they do not suffer while the Sacrifice is being offered on their behalf. Let us therefore remember very often the souls of our friends, and of all the faithful departed.

After that the priest joins to the commemoration of the Church suffering that of the Church militant (*Nobis quoque peccatoribus*) and of the Church triumphant. He prays that the Church militant may be admitted into the company of the elect, not through their own scanty merits but through the superabundance of the Lord's mercy.

And then come some more of the elect: it is a continuation of the list of martyrs, begun a while ago in the *Communicantes*.

First comes *John the Baptist*, the prosecutor, who prepared the way of the Lord with the most severe penance and the most sincere humility.

Stephen, the Protomartyr, who showed such nobility in asking pardon for those who were barbarously stoning him to death.

The apostle *Matthias*, who was elected as against Joseph, surnamed Justus, and was numbered in the apostolic college after the treachery of Judas Iscariot.

The disciple *Barnabas*, Saint Paul's companion in his preaching for twelve years. Afterwards he continued his apostolic activity until he was stoned to death as a blasphemer. He was buried with Saint Matthew's gospel which he was accustomed to carry about with him.

Ignatius, bishop of Antioch, who wrote: 'I am God's grain and I am to be ground by the teeth of the wild beasts, to make me into pure bread.'

Alexander, who succeeded Evaristus as pope and occupied the Holy See for approximately ten years.

Marcellinus, a priest, and *Peter*, an exorcist, were condemned to death. They were taken to a forest about three miles outside Rome and there beheaded.

Then come two martyrs who were married: *Perpetua* and *Felicity*. The former was a mother and the latter was with child at the time when they were thrown to the wild beasts.

Let us, like them, martyr our body and our soul so that we may attain that *perpetual felicity* of which, as Saint Augustine says, the happy association of their names makes us think.

Finally, five virgin martyrs:

Agatha, whose breasts were cut off because she refused to surrender her honour to Quintianus, a man of consular rank. She was miraculously healed by Saint Peter the apostle. Her virginal veil, which was covering her tomb, several times extinguished the lava which fell down in fiery torrents from Mount Etna, threatening to burn the whole city. That is how God honoured the heroic resistance she offered against the assaults of the passions.

Lucy who, enlightened with a light from on high, declared to her judge that 'pure hearts are temples of the Holy Ghost.' She, in fact, showed that the light of purity burned brightly in the temple of her soul and she heroically guarded it to the end.

And we ... are we to continue in darkness?

Agnes, scarcely thirteen years old, said to her executioner: 'Strike the blow without fear, for a bride would offend her bridegroom if she kept him waiting.'

Cecilia, born of a noble family, consecrated her virginity to God when she was a child. Forced to marry a pagan named Valerian, on the night of the wedding she said to him: 'Do not dare to touch me. For I have an angel who guards my virginity.' The husband decided to be baptized and then he saw the angel as she did...

Anastasia was martyred at Sirmium in Dalmatia, probably under the persecution of Diocletian. In the old Roman liturgy, the second Mass on Christmas Day was of this saint, but nowadays there is only a commemoration of her.

All these were victims, chosen by God to confound the powerful of this world who are so full of themselves!

With that great veneration should we recall your names and your outstanding virtues, in order to imitate them in this world, so that afterwards, in the next, we may enjoy your blessed company!

AND NOW WE HAVE ARRIVED AT THE SOLEMN CON-clusion of the Canon, the *Per ipsum*.

It is a very concise formula, but so significant that we must spend some time considering it.

X
Actio IV: Doxology

'THROUGH HIM, AND WITH HIM, AND IN HIM...'
At the end of all the Church's prayers we find the words: *Per Christum Dominum nostrum,* through Jesus Christ our Lord. Christ is truly the way.

And the prayer *par excellence,* the Canon ends with the formula: 'Through him, and with him, and in him, be to thee, God the Father almighty, in the unity of the holy Ghost, all honour and glory.' 'Mystical theology, which must be respected,' says D. Vandeur,[1] 'venerates this formula as the most profound expression of the glorification of the adorable Trinity and a sublime expression of the offering of Jesus Christ made to it.'

'Thus,' says the Council of Trent,[2] 'man has not wherein to glory, but all our glorifying is in Christ: in whom we merit, in whom we satisfy, "bringing forth fruits worthy of penance" which from him have their efficacy, by him are offered to the Father and through him are accepted by the Father.'

It is through him, with him and in him that the members of the mystical Body, of which he is the head, fulfill their first and fundamental duty of giving perfect praise to the blessed Trinity.

For 'he alone, who is the creator of all things, the head and king of all creatures, is capable of offering God complete satisfaction.

'His is the only voice which can penetrate from this world to the throne of the divine majesty, the only eloquent word which can pierce the heavens; only he truly prays and

---

[1] *La sainte Messe,* p. 247.
[2] Session XIV, C.VIII.

beseeches in the name of all living beings; he is our only interpreter, our advocate, our Priest.'[3]

The mystical Body of Christ... A sublime doctrine! A miracle of love!

Let us read Saint Paul, through whose mouth, as Pope Saint Leo said, Christ himself speaks:

'For as in one body we have many members, but all the members have not the same office; so we, being many, are one body in Christ; and every one members one of another; and having different gifts, according to the grace that is given us.'[4]

And in another passage the great apostle writes: 'The body also is not one member, but many... If they all were one member, where would be the body?'

'For as the body is one and hath many members; and all the members of the body, whereas they are many, yet are one body; so also is Christ.'[5] This is the union of the faithful with Christ and Christ with the faithful. From this a most important conclusion follows: 'If one member suffer any thing, all the members suffer with it; or, if one member glory, all the members rejoice with it!'

And the apostle continues: 'You are the body of Christ and members of member.'[6]

Christ is the Head of this mystical Body: 'God... made him the head to which the whole Church is joined, so that the Church is his body, the completion of him who everywhere and in all things is complete.'[7]

Again: 'Such a man... is not united to that head of ours, on whom all the body depends, supplied and unified by joint and ligament, and so growing up with a growth which is divine.'[8] That is to say: the mystical Body receives from its

[3] Cf, Abbé C. Grimaud: *Ma Messe*, p. 82.
[4] Romans XII, 4-6.
[5] I Corinthians XII, 12, 14 and 19.
[6] I Corinthians XII, 26 and 27.
[7] Ephesians I, 22-23.
[8] Colossians II, 19.

Head, which is Jesus Christ, the divine life which circulates through it all.

But if some member does not adhere to the Head, then Christ's warning will apply to him: 'If any one abide not in me, he shall be cast forth as a branch and shall wither.'[9] It will receive no more sap; it will no longer have any divine life in it.

And what greater misfortune can there be than this? For how are those members to advance if they have no light? They will certainly lose their way. Of what use are their eyes if they have no light to show them the way? Poor souls! My friend, let us go out to meet them.

But there is another thing: at times it is necessary to die that others may live. Do not forget that!

If your death means their redemption it will mean your redemption also.

Let us think of this very often: if one member is ill all the others suffer with it. How careful we must be then, not to do anything which might harm the mystical Body!

But if one member is honoured, all the others share in its joy. That is to say: if a soul rises up, it raises the world with it. What an incitement to perfection! That thought should certainly broaden our heart and our mind, and make us often think of *the whole Body*.

From this moment on let us make a resolution: I am going to advance in virtue so that the whole Body may advance.

That is the Communion of Saints.

THROUGH HIM.

'I am the Way.'

One of the reasons why many souls make little progress in the spiritual life is that they have no understanding of God's plan for them, or they make no effort to adapt themselves to that plan.

---

9 John XV, 6.

'The more I get to know souls,' says D. Columba Marmion, 'the more I become convinced that even to know this divine plan is itself a great grace, that to have recourse to it is a source of unceasing outpourings of divine grace and that to adapt ourselves to it is the very essence of sanctity.

'Now, this divine plan can be stated in a few words: to re-establish all things in Christ. That is to say: God wants to give us everything, he wants to give everything to all of us, but he gives it only *through* Christ, *with* Christ and *in* Christ. In short: Christ is the only way. Therefore, if we are to find God, all we have to do is follow Christ by accepting and practicing his doctrine and imitating his example.'

WITHOUT HIM YOU CAN DO NOTHING.

With him, in him, you can do all things.

'The Divine life in us is only a participation, by grace, in that fulness of life which is in the Humanity of Christ Jesus, and flows in each of our souls to make us children of God: *De plenitudine ejus nos omnes accepimus* (Jn. I, 16). The source of our holiness is there and not elsewhere. This holiness... is of an essentially supernatural order; we shall only find it in our union with Jesus Christ: *Sine me nihil potestis facere* (Jn. XV, 5). All the treasures of grace and of holiness that God destines for souls are gathered up in Jesus Christ; He came here below to give us a share in these treasures... So that, if without Him we can do nothing, in Him we are made rich, and nothing is wanting to us: *Ita ut nihil vobis desit in ulla gratia.*'[10]

Without him you can do nothing; do not rely on your own strength. But with him you can do everything: with him and through him, your prayers, your efforts and all your actions, are of great value. Therefore in the moment of temptation do not lose courage: continue with your good works.

10 D. Marmion: *Christ the Life of the Soul*, pp. 267-8.

Do not say: What use is working, struggling, when I see no fruit, no results? You can do all things in him who strengthens you. And besides, it is for him to give the fruits. What you have to do is sow good seed... Later he will do the rest, as he thinks fit. His will is always the best.

Undoubtedly it is difficult to go on working without seeing any of the expected fruits. But that is of no importance, if it is what the Lord wants. Work only because he wants it. And in this alone you should have sufficient consolation.

WITH HIM.

'I am the Truth.'

He who is with Jesus is on the path of truth. Pity those poor people who are separated from him, in the shadows of error.

Therefore, my friend, give thanks to God that one day he gave you knowledge of the truth and that now you can rest in it.

Perhaps once you had to disperse from your soul the darkness left in it by a sterile rationalism. And when the rays of light shone down on your brain, tell me, my friend, did you not feel as if everything in your mind were turned upside down... that a brightness, never before seen, illuminated your intelligence and opened up for it new and unexpected horizons? Did you not feel that brightness dispersing all the shadows and, as if by magic, ridding you of many disturbing doubts? A great grace, my friend, a great grace!

What an enormous joy... in being conquered!

How sublime it was... to conquer!

So now, do not sleep. Excel all others in devotion. Rise up. He, the Lord, gave you a new life. And you, what do you give Him?'

My friend, always be very truthful in your actions. Let everything you do be full of truth. Your whole life must conform to the fact that you are a creature, free and rational, subject to the will of God; to the fact that you are a son of God with your own special vocation, with your own individuality.[11]

Lie neither to God nor to men. You say that people consider you something other than what you are in reality? Have patience. Bear everything for love of him who, although the Saint above all saints, was considered to be everything that is worst and was treated as such. He knows exactly what you are in reality. He will see that you get justice one day. Men have no power to judge you. Be very upright always, very straightforward, despite all contradictions.

It is extremely important, for your spiritual good, that you should wish to be what you are, with your own character and your own qualities.

'In our supernatural life we must preserve of our personality whatever is good in it.'[12]

'Holiness is not a single mould where the natural qualities that characterise one's personality have to disappear so that only a uniform type may be represented. Far from that. God, in creating us, endowed each of us with gifts, talents, privileges; each soul has its special natural beauty: one shines by

---

11 'In order to act as Christians, we must first of all act as men. And this is not without importance. Doubtless, a perfect Christian will necessarily fulfill his duties as man, for the law of the Gospel comprises and perfects the natural law. But one meets with Christians, or rather with some calling themselves Christians, and that not only among the simple faithful, but even among religious and priests, who are exact even to scrupulosity as to their self-chosen practices of piety, and yet hold certain precepts of the natural law very cheaply. These people have it at heart not to miss their exercises of devotion, and this is excellent, but, for example, they do not refrain from attacking a neighbor's reputation, from telling falsehoods, and failing to keep their word; they do not scruple to give a wrong meaning to what an author has written nor to infringe the laws of literary or artistic property; they defer, sometimes to the detriment of justice, the payment of their debts, and are not exact in observing the clauses of a contract.' D. Marmion: *Christ the Life of the Soul*, p. 206.

12 Regarding your defects: 'you should not cherish them or love them, but bear them patiently, for often they are very good for you because they let you see your misery.' St. Francis de Sales: *Letter to Mme. De Chantal.*

depth of intelligence, another is distinguished by strength of will, a third attracts by breadth of charity. Grace respects this beauty as it respects the nature on which it is based; it will but add a supernatural splendour to the natural beauty, enhancing and transfiguring it. In His sanctifying operation, God respects his work of creation, for he has willed this diversity: each soul, in translating one of the Divine thoughts, has a special place in the heart of God.'[13]

Do not say: If I were like this or like that I would do this great thing or that great thing, I would become a saint quite easily...

You are what you are, nothing more and nothing less. All the rest are flights of fancy which only destroy all the efforts you should be making *at this very moment* to correct your faults and to increase in virtue. Once you start dreaming of better situations, you cease trying to *improve* the situation in which you are at present.

Saint Benedict advises his sons to have no desire to be considered holy before they are so.[14]

Of what benefit would those lies be to us? Do you think that those false judgements of men can make us saints?

How can they give what they have not got?

So, my friend, let us be convinced together with Saint Teresa that it is indeed great humility for each one of us to be contented with the place which the Lord destined for him in life. That is where we must sanctify ourselves.

IN HIM.

'I am Life.'

Jesus possesses in himself the fulness of all grace. 'As the Father has within him the gift of life, so he has granted to the Son that he too should have within him the gift of life'

---

13 D. Marmion: *Christ the Life of the Soul*, p. 208.
14 *Rule*, chap IV, 61.

(Jn. V, 26). And this life is eternal life, a vast ocean of divine life which includes all the perfections and all the beatitude of the divinity.

Christ possesses this divine life in himself, of his very nature, of his own right, because he is the Son of God, the Word made flesh. Much more than that: he *is* life.

Now Jesus wants us to share that life which he himself possesses in all its fulness: 'I come that they may have life and have it more abundantly.'

He wants that life, which is his through the hypostatic union, to be ours through grace. It is of his fulness that we must all receive it.

There is no grace which is not found in Jesus as its source, for in him all the treasures of divine knowledge and wisdom are hidden. And they are to be transmitted to us through him.

Therefore if we wish — and we must wish — to have life, *to live*, we must be united to him. Without him we can do nothing, but with him, in him, we can bear much fruit.

Therefore let us do exactly what he wants us to do, for the best way of remaining united to him is to be united to his holy will. In order to be a saint it is essential always and everywhere to do his will.

Saint Benedict wants the profession of his monks to be made in union with Jesus' Sacrifice, with the Sacrifice of the altar. It is Christ who gives value to their oblation.

In the same way too our sufferings and voluntary mortifications are of value only in so far as they are united, through faith and love, to those of Jesus.

We must be convinced that perfection does not consist in exterior mortifications, even very severe and extraordinary ones, if they are done only for their own sake. What we must do is abandon ourselves to them, bear patiently the sufferings which come to us every day, and accept them for love of our Lord and in union with his blessed Passion.

As Louis de Blois says, we must unite everything we

Actio IV: Doxology

do and everything we suffer to the deeds and sufferings of Christ. In this way all our actions and all our trials, in themselves miserable and worthless, become enormous and very pleasing to God, because the merits of Christ, to which they are united, give them an unmeasurable dignity. 'We can be saints only according to the measure in which the life of Jesus Christ is in us.'[15] Do not forget that.

To sum up: Christ is the only *Way*, and if men walk outside of that way they will be lost for eternity; he is the infallible *Truth*, outside of which there is only error and darkness; he is the one true *Life*, he will deliver us from death, he is the living Life.

It is through him, and with him, and in him that all honour and glory is given to thee, O God the Father almighty, in the unity of the holy Ghost.

---

15   D. Marmion: *Christ the Life of the Soul*, p. 38.

XI
The Kiss of Peace

THE KISS OF PEACE, WHICH IS GIVEN AT SOLEMN Masses, is symbolic of that charity which should unite all those who approach the altar.

From the very beginning of the Church, love was always the characteristic of the disciples of Jesus, and he was the vital principle of their unity. They expressed and fostered their love with a kiss, a kiss of unsullied purity, enlivened with all the supernatural affections of their soul. A kiss of love, a kiss of peace: for love begets peace.

Formerly the kiss of peace was given before the Offertory as a farewell to the Catechumens, and in order to prepare the faithful for the oblation. But soon it came to be considered as an excellent preparation for the Communion and was then placed before the breaking of the bread.

Later the breaking of the bread was brought forward and the kiss of peace remained before the prayers which immediately precede the Communion.

Before giving the kiss of peace, the celebrant kisses the altar, which represents Jesus. If he is a prelate, he then gives the kiss to the assisting priest, deacons and ministers; if he is a priest, he gives it to the assisting priest if there is one, otherwise to the deacon, who transmits it to the subdeacon, and he in turn gives it to the choir and the lower ministers.

Originally the kiss was given and received on the lips. Nowadays it is given to the clergy by an embrace. He who gives it says: 'Peace be to you,' and he who receives it answers: 'And with thy spirit.' The subdeacon gives the kiss to the laity in order of dignity, by giving them an appropriate instrument, the pax or osculatory, to kiss.

IMMEDIATELY AFTER THE KISS OF PEACE WE HAVE the beautiful prayer *ad pacem*: 'O Lord Jesus Christ, who saidst to thy apostles, Peace I leave with you, my peace I give unto you; look not on my sins, but on the faith of thy Church; and vouchsafe to grant her that peace and unity which is agreeable to thy will: O God who livest and reignest for ever and ever. Amen.'

What a beautiful prayer that is: it asks first and foremost for peace for the *whole* Church!

Indeed, liturgical prayer always has regard to the collectivity, the society, the mystical Body. The priest asks the Lord to regard not his own *personal* sins but the faith of the *whole* mystical Body, the faith of his Church. He asks him not to regard him separately, but in union with all the faithful, as a member of that mystical Body of which he, Jesus, is the Head.

Let us open wide our heart; let us broaden the horizons of our piety. Let our prayer be social, let the liturgical prayer be our prayer... Let us live the Communion of Saints! The Lord did not teach us to say '*My* father' but '*Our* Father,' 'Give *us* this day...' not 'Give *me*.'

PEACE! HOW OFTEN A FRIENDLY WORD, A SMILE, A little interest shown, in any form whatever, in one of our brothers, will do his soul a world of good, dry up a torrent of contemptuous thoughts, quiet a tempest in his heart, perhaps encourage him to persevere and... restore peace!

My friend: your religion must be very true; that is to say: you must be as scrupulous in respecting the reputation of others, in fulfilling your word, whatever it costs, as you are in fulfilling your pious duties. Your active life must be an overflow of your interior life. Do not be one of those people who think they can please God merely by faithfulness — often purely exterior — to their pious duties and devotions... while they have neither tolerance nor charity towards their neighbor; they cover his name in defamation and in mud; they refuse to forgive those who go humbly to ask their pardon.

Always be in agreement, as much as possible, with your brothers, provided your duties to God do not suffer. They have their own character, their own principles, their own way of looking at things, their own way of living; and you have yours. Make an effort. Go to them full of pity and compassion for their defects, determined to be tolerant of them all. Open up your heart. There are undoubtedly many things in common, many points of contact, between you and them. Try to find those points.

But go even further than that: sacrifice your own personal views and tastes and, with a loving delicacy, try to please theirs. Put yourself in their place; step into their shoes. Imitate Saint Paul who said: 'To the weak I became weak, that I might gain the weak. I became all things to all men, that I might save all' (I Cor. IX, 20-22). You will see how they come closer to you, how their hearts will join with your heart, in a deep love and friendship.

Thus you will have peace in your own heart and in your relations with your brothers—peace born of generosity.

IN DISTURBANCES AND IN CALM, IN INTERIOR DRYness and in sensible consolation, in fervour and in aridity, in a word: in every state of soul and in all the circumstances of life, you must try to keep your will closely united to the will of God, to regard whatever happens to you as the best, since whatever happens to you comes from him. Thus you will have peace in your heart.

And never let sadness or gloom enter into your heart. Sadness: why? Whatever happens to you is God's will, and he wishes only your good. To be sad is useless; it saps all one's energy.

Rejoice always in the Lord: for he 'loves the cheerful giver.'

Repentance is a very good thing, but it must be accomplished by great serenity and great peace, great confidence in the Lord's infinite mercy. It has been said that fear is the beginning of wisdom. The beginning, yes, but the culmination of wisdom is love. There are times, I know, when the devil wants to see you downhearted and he suggests that you stop praying and give up all pious practices.

Do not let yourself be fooled. These suggestions are familiar to us: no divine inspiration will ever propose such things.

No, do not be deceived, do not give in to that temptation but at those times pray more than ever, even though you find it very difficult and you do not feel any inclination to pray. Do *everything possible* to pray properly, attentively and devoutly; and you can be assured that thus your prayer is of great value; it is even more valuable than when it is accompanied by sensible consolation; it is then completely pure.

Wait patiently. Very soon heavenly dew will fall on the dry earth. And even if it never comes, praise God for those trials which he sends you; be faithful in his service, confident in the knowledge that he who perseveres to the end will be saved.

XII

Kiss of Love: Communion

*'O wondrous gift indeed!
The poor and lowly may
Upon their Lord and Master feed.'*[1]

IT HAS BEEN SAID, AND IT IS WORTH REPEATING, that shepherds eat the flesh of their lambs, whereas Jesus alone, the Good Shepherd, gives himself to be eaten by his.

Furthermore: 'When we assimilate the food of the body, we change it into our own substance, whilst Christ gives himself to us in order to transform us into himself.'[2] Christ wants to be the principle behind all the interior activity of the soul; he wants to operate in it, in us. And if the soul surrenders itself with docility to his influence Christ becomes the life of that soul, which in turn becomes transformed little by little into him whom it loves: *Vivo ego jam non ego, vivit vero in me Christus.* 'I live, now not I, but Christ liveth in me.'

Ah, how logical it would be if we always went around with our hands joined! But at least let our heart be always ready to soar on high in acts of thanksgiving.

At the purification of our Lady, when old Simeon took the child Jesus in his arms and shouted with joy, he was overwhelmed with happiness.

And we, who take him into our heart every day, how lukewarm we are, how coldly we receive him!

Yes. We envy, with a holy envy, the disciple whom Jesus loved, because he was able to recline on the Lord's breast.

---

1 From the hymn *Sacris solemniis*.
2 D. Marmion: *Christ the Life of the Soul*, p. 265.

And we can have him every day *within ourselves*. Consider well, my friend, what a great honour it is to be able to receive, as a guest in our soul, the Lord of all things.

'Acknowledge, Christian, your great dignity,' said Pope Saint Leo. Think: God dwells in our soul!

We must be convinced that it is 'not only in order that we may adore him, and offer him to his father as infinite satisfaction, that Christ renders himself present on the altar; it is not only to visit us that he comes, but it is that we may eat him as the Food of our souls, and that eating him, we may have life, the life of grace here below, the life of glory hereafter.'[3]

But he is not only the food for the soul. ' He also nourishes our body and is a salutary remedy for its failings,' says Saint Teresa. And the priest, before Communion, asks that the partaking of the body of the Lord Jesus Christ may be 'a safeguard and a healing remedy both of soul and body.'

'TASTE, AND SEE THAT THE LORD IS SWEET.'

Come, all of you: he is the bread of life.

He, the Lord God, gives himself: do you not want to receive him?...Your faults...I know. But his mercy is infinitely greater than your faults.

Besides, he knows them better than you do and, in spite of that, even because of that,[4] he wishes to live in you. He wants to be united intimately with you. Obey promptly and think of nothing else. I know: the devil is very interested in those false demonstrations of respect, because he does not want you to be united to him who is life itself. Do not listen to him. Listen only to the Lord who is calling

---

[3] D. Marmion: *Christ the Life of the Soul*, p. 262.
[4] 'It is your miseries which draw down his grace upon you. Where there is no misery, neither is their place for mercy. So that your miseries, confessed with humility, are the title you can show in order to claim the divine mercy.' D. I. Van Houtryve: *A Vida na Paz* ed. p. 160.

you. Obey his invitation with all simplicity; with filial fear, certainly, for we are poor creatures, full of defects and sins; but never with servile fear, for that would be an insult to present the Lord's infinite goodness. God is our father, a most loving father.

'In the Incarnation, the Word associated all humanity to his mysteries and to his Person, by a mystical union.

'If our Lord has willed to make himself present under the species of bread and wine, it is in order to become our Food. And if we seek to know why Christ willed to institute this Sacrament under the form of food, we see that it is first of all to maintain the divine life within us; next, in order that, receiving this divine life from him, we may remain united to him.'[5] Now, the Word, when he became man, did always what was pleasing to his heavenly Father: *quae placita sunt ei facio semper.* So that to go to Mass and not to receive holy Communion is a refusal to fulfill completely the desires of Christ and the hopes of our Father in heaven.[6]

In the early days of the Church everyone who attended Mass received holy Communion. Sometimes, as a punishment for some offence, a person was forbidden to receive. 'And when he who presides has celebrated the Eucharist they whom we call deacons permit each one present to partake of the Eucharistic bread, and wine and water; and they carry it also to the absentees.'[7] The sick, the prisoners and the martyrs were not forgotten. When the faithful receive holy Communion during the Mass at which they assist, they imitate and represent in an adequate manner that sacred act of holy Thursday. At the last supper, Jesus united himself to his

---

5   D. Marmion: *Christ the Life of the Soul*, pp. 255, 261.
6   The Council of Trent formulated this desire: 'The sacred and holy Synod would fain indeed that, at each Mass, the faithful who are present should communicate, not only in spiritual desire, but also by the sacramental participation of the Eucharist, that thereby a more abundant fruit might be derived to them from this most holy sacrifice.' (Session XXII, ch. VI).
7   St. Justin: *First Apology*, ch. 65.

apostles by participating in one and the same sacrifice: they ate the same bread, they drank of the same chalice, and thus the union between the disciples and their Master was sealed.

From this we see that Jesus wanted the holy Eucharist to be a sign of unity in the Catholic Church, both to unite the faithful among themselves, and to unite them to their hierarchic superiors. So that if the faithful receive Communion during Mass, it fosters that unity between Christians much more than does Communion received outside the holy Sacrifice.[8]

Certainly holy Communion is received, and we are permitted to receive it, outside Mass, but this should be done only in exceptional cases; and even then we should always unite our holy Communion, at least by intention, to the holy Mass.

It is certain that if we continually separate holy Communion from Mass, we run the risk of losing all sense of the full significance of the Host, we deprive ourselves of the grace which comes from following the example of Christ in this most wonderful sacrifice which is offered every day on our patens, and which invites us to unite ourselves with him, and consummate our offering in him.

PREPARATION FOR HOLY COMMUNION: ITS NECESSITY

It is true that the Sacraments of themselves produce the result for which they were instituted, but on condition that no obstacle is put in their way: *non ponentibus obicem*.

---

[8] 'It is very important that the faithful should take part in the Sacrifice by offering themselves at the Offertory, at least spiritually, and as often as possible by communicating sacramentally after the celebrant. The reason for saying "as often as possible" is that, although it is desirable that the faithful should communicate during Mass not only out of respect for the liturgy but also in order to share more intimately in the Sacrifice and to profit by the preparation and thanksgiving which the Church obliges the celebrant to make, still it would be a pity if, out of a kind of pharisaical severity, the faithful, who sometimes cannot communicate at the liturgical moment, were to be deprived outside Mass of the Communion which the Church advises them to receive every day.' Coelho: *O que é a Liturgia*, p. 47.

Now, on the part of Christ there can be no obstacle, for in him are all the treasures of the divinity, and he desires, with an infinite desire, to give us those treasures by coming to us himself; he came to give us life and he wishes us to have it in abundance.

The only obstacles, then, are in us. Everything opposed to our supernatural life and to our union with Christ is an obstacle to our reaping the fruits of the Eucharist.

Consequently the first necessity is that we should be in the state of grace. 'Together with a "right intention", this is the first condition for the faithful to be able to approach Christ and receive the Bread of Life.'[9] That was decreed by the great Pope Pius X, in a memorable document concerning frequent Communion.[10]

REMOTE PREPARATION

There is a very important *general disposition*, a consequence of the mere nature of any union, which is an admirable preparation for our union with Jesus Christ, and, above all, for the perfection of that union: that is *complete* and often renewed self-surrender of ourselves to Jesus Christ.

This surrender of ourselves to the Word made man began with Baptism. It was in Baptism that, through grace, we began to resemble God, to be united to him. Now, the more we continue in that original disposition of death to sin and life to God, the better prepared will we be, in a remote way, to receive the abundance of Eucharistic grace.

What are the obstacles to the perfection of this union? These are our bad habits which we know of and which we do not correct; voluntary attachment to ourselves and to creatures.

This is especially true of deliberate or habitual faults against charity towards our neighbour.

---

9   D. Marmion: *Christ the Life of the Soul*, p. 269.
10 Decree of 20th Dec. 1905.

True, it is not our dispositions which *produce* the grace of the sacrament, for the sacraments confer grace *ex opere operato*; but our dispositions allow the sacraments to work freely, they remove the obstacles. We must open up our hearts, as widely as possible, and allow the divine gifts to enter.

Therefore, another excellent disposition is to try never to refuse Christ anything.

The Eucharist is the sacrament of union, as the word *Communion* indicates. But to *unite* is to make of two things one single thing. Now, Communion represents the sacrifice of the altar, therefore the sacrifice of the Cross. That is to say: in Holy Communion, Christ makes us share in his own sacrifice; we become victims with him.

Therefore we must try to become like Christ, the victim. A soul which is thus disposed for union, prepared to give itself *without reserve*, tolerates no obstacles; and when God does not find obstacles in a soul he works wonders for the sanctity of that soul.

It is for lack of this disposition towards union — this *dispositio unionis* — that many souls make little or no progress in the way of perfection, in spite of frequent holy Communion. Now, since this disposition is of such great value, we should ask the Lord earnestly to help us to acquire it and keep it. 'Ask and you shall receive.'

Let us, therefore, pray with the priest: 'Cleanse our thoughts, we beseech thee, O Lord, by thy visitation, that when our Lord Jesus Christ, thy Son, shall come, he may find within us a dwelling prepared for him.'

PROXIMATE PREPARATION[11]

The ceremony of the Kiss of peace is immediately followed by the two prayers *Domine Jesu Christe*... and *Perceptio*... which are recited as a preparation for holy Communion. They are very personal prayers, and the priest bows

---

11 Strictly speaking, the *proximate* preparation begins with the *Pater Noster*. What we deal with here, then, should more properly be called the *immediate* preparation.

Kiss of Love: Communion

down reverently, with his eyes placed on the sacred host to which these prayers are addressed.

The priest asks Jesus in the host to deliver him from all sins and from all kinds of evil, never to permit him to transgress his commandments, and never to be separated from him.

Yes, we are indeed unfortunate if we lose him!

For how can a blind man walk in the dark? The way to achieve final perseverance is to be faithful everyday. By practicing the *virtue* of perseverance we shall obtain the *gift* of final perseverance.[12]

What an inestimable gift, what an incomparable gift, is that of *final perseverance*. And there are many souls who lose this excellent opportunity of asking the Lord for it.

Then the priest, more convinced than ever of his unworthiness, humbly asks the Lord that this Communion may not be a cause of his judgement and damnation, but that, through God's goodness, it may be a safeguard and a healing remedy for his soul and body. Why should we not recite these beautiful prayers with the priest, especially if we communicate sacramentally, as is desirable, for they dispose us better than any other prayers for receiving the Sacrament?[13]

---

12 'Perseverance is, in fact, the virtue that consummates and crowns all the others. We must be careful to distinguish this *virtue* of perseverance from the *gift* of final perseverance, which allows us to "die in the Lord": this gift is purely gratuitous and the Council of Trent says that "no one can be sure, absolutely sure, that it will be granted him" (Session VI, ch. 13). However, the holy Council adds: "we ought to have and to keep the most lively confidence in God's help, for God is all-powerful to bring to completion in us the good which he has begun, unless we ourselves are unfaithful to his grace." (*Ibid.*) The means, then, given to us in order that we may count upon this infinitely precious gift, the gift exceeding all others, is daily fidelity; and we shall carry out well and to its end the great each work that we undertake for God: this is the object of the virtue of perseverance.' D. Marmion: *Christ the Ideal of the Monk*, p. 143.

13 'When possible, this is the best immediate preparation for receiving Christ. In thus preparing ourselves, we are united more directly to the Sacrifice of Christ and to the intentions of his Sacred Heart ... As to the *formulae* to help us in the immediate preparation for this union with Jesus, one cannot fix on any exclusively, the needs of souls as well as their aptitudes being so varied.' D. Marmion: *Christ the Life of the Soul*, p. 278.

Let us then, be detached from all vanity, from love of self, from all exaggerated sensitivity. Let us die to ourselves.

Furthermore: let us, every day, by an explicit, real act, relate all our actions to our Communion. This is an excellent practice.

Saint Francis de Sales, when he was ordained, made a resolution to convert every moment of every day into a preparation for the following day's Eucharistic Sacrifice, so that he could reply truthfully at any moment, if he were asked what he was doing: 'I am preparing to celebrate Mass.'

PREPARATION FOR COMMUNION!

'There are few who perceive within themselves the admirable effects of this sacred Banquet, because there are few who rightly dispose themselves to receive them, who seriously reflect that they approach the Holy of Holies, the Altar of God, God Himself.'[14]

Put aside all the cares of this world!

Let us bring with us from the world only those holy intentions for which we are going to pray. Interior preparation above all. But do not despise the exterior: neatness in our own person and in the things of the Church; a grave and modest attitude; fidelity in the smallest details, not out of scruples, but *out of love*. Let us remember that nothing is little in the sight of our God and that the most humble ceremony has an enormous value in his divine eyes.

Christ is the host! Let us be hosts with him. Let us determine to refuse him nothing. Let us put no obstacles in the way of his sanctifying influence.

Lord, I am not worthy...

'We must not forget that the holy Spirit breathes where he will and that therefore piety takes many varied forms, even in the same person. Thus what inspires devotion in some people will distract or upset others and, even in one and the same person, a religious practice which formerly helped him to advance in union with God may later plunge him into a state of dryness and sterility.' Antonio Coelho: *O que é a Liturgia*, p. 67.

14 Cardinal Bona: *De Missae celebratione*, ch. III, I.

But who can be worthy of such great mercy? Lord, show me my hidden sins and forgive all the others. If you were to take note of all our iniquities, Lord, who could stand safely in your presence?

Unhappy is he who dares to appear at the banquet without a wedding garment!

Besides, the Lord does not come to us because of any merit on our part. He is the bread of life, of which our poor soul has vital need: *Caro mea vere est cibus*...

And the soul approaches as one who is sick, to the physician of life, as one unclean, to the fountain of mercy, as one blind, to the light of eternal brightness, as one poor and needy, to the Lord of heaven and earth.[15]

Unworthy!

Let us hear Saint Gertrude, that gentle herald of the divine love, in whose writings souls thirsty for interior life can find valuable lessons. One morning she was preparing for holy Communion and a few moments before the great event she began this soliloquy: 'Behold, thy spouse calls thee: and how canst thou dare to appear before him without being adorned as thou shouldst be?'

And on seeing her own unworthiness, her soul began to be clouded with mistrust of her own good works. But that lasted only a moment; it was only a slight movement in her soul... and then a high wave of confidence swelled and overflowed in it in such a way that she abandoned herself completely, without a trace of fear, into the hands of the infinite Love, and exclaimed: 'Why defer longer? Since, even had I a thousand years, I could not prepare as I ought, having nothing which could serve to promote the right dispositions in me. But I will meet him with confidence and humility, and when my Lord beholds me from afar, he can fill me with all the grace and the attractions with which his love desires that I should appear before him.'[16]

15 Prayer of St. Thomas Aquinas.
16 Saint Gertrude: *Revelations*, part III, ch. XVII, 5.

And then... it is the Word of God who speaks to her: 'The more unworthy of divine favours he may be towards whom the Word of God inclines lovingly, all the more triumphant will be the song with which creatures exalt the mercy of the Lord.' 'But,' interrupted the saint, 'surely he who, seeing his own unworthiness, hesitates to receive your most pure Body, gives testimony of the respect he has for such a noble sacrament.' And Christ answered: 'My daughter, he who receives me with the intention which I have told you — that is the desire of my glory — he will never be lacking in the reverence which is my due.'

Then Christ said more in order to banish all such shyness: 'Since I find my delight in dwelling with the children of men, and have left them this Sacrament by an excess of love for a remembrance of me, that by this they may remember me frequently; and, finally, have obliged myself to remain in this mystery until the consummation of ages — all who, by their words or persuasions, drive away those who are not in mortal sin, hinder and interrupt the delight which I find in them.'[17]

LORD, I AM NOT WORTHY...

Do not say: I am worthy of nothing; I am absolutely miserable.

If, some day, someone were to take your words literally... perhaps the same thing would happen to you as happened to a certain devout lady whom Saint Francis de Sales purposely treated as if she were in reality what her false humility made her say she was.[18] You might not like it very much.

Humility does not know that it is humble, it is forbidden from itself; therefore it does not say, it cannot say, that it is humble.

To think that one is humble shows a lack of humility.[19]

17 *Ibid.* ch. LXVI.
18 Cf. *The Spirit of St. Francis de Sales*, VIII, II.
19 ' I do not term humility, that ceremonious profusion of words, gestures and kissings of the ground, obeisances, inclinations, when they are made, as often

'It is very important,' says Dom Van Houtryve, 'not to think you have attained humility, because even to think that is a strong indication that it is not true.'

It is Saint Francis de Sales who says: 'Very often we say that we are nothing, that we are only miserable wretches.

'But we would be very amazed if people took us literally, if they judged us or declared us to be what we say we are...We pretend to flee from honour and hide ourselves...but secretly hoping that we will be found.

'We act as if we really wanted to be the last of all, we sit in the lowest place at the banquet table...with a deep and lively, although hidden, desire of being invited to go up higher.'

You too, my friend, ardently desire that the divine Word should be united with you. But if your desire is *really* ardent, it must be effective, active, it must make you destroy everything in yourself which is opposed to that union. Otherwise it will be false like the desire of those minds 'that find admirable — as indeed it is — what they call the "positive side" of the spiritual life: love, prayer, contemplation, union with God, but forget that all this is only to be found with certainty in a soul purified from all sin, from all evil habits, and which constantly tends, by a life of generous vigilance, to abate the sources of sin and imperfection. The spiritual edifice is very fragile when it is not based upon the constant flight from sin, for it is built upon sand.'[20]

JESUS IS OUR BEST FRIEND!

You must get used to telling him, with the confidence and simplicity of a child, everything your heart feels: joys and sorrows, all those doubts which torment you, all those

---

happens, without any inward sense of our own abjection and of just esteem of our neighbor: for all this is but a vain occupation of weak brains, and is rather to be termed a phantom of humility, than humility itself. I speak of a noble, real, productive and solid humility, which makes us supple to correction, pliable and prompt to obedience.' St. Francis de Sales: *Treatise on the Love of God*, Bk. VIII, ch. XIII.
20 D. Marmion: *Christ, the Ideal of the Monk*, A, VIII.

periods of enthusiasm, fervour and interior dryness—in a word: everything. Go to him and tell him everything, often. Does not the psalmist say: 'Pour out your hearts before him'? (Ps. LXI, 9)

If only you knew how much he likes you to confide in him!

It is true that he knows very well what you have to say: he sees the most intimate corner of your heart and there is nothing hidden from him. But he wants you to tell all to him, to look for him, to desire him.

And if you go to your friends to open your heart to them and tell them all your secrets, which perhaps they will not understand very well, and which at times they will betray, either intentionally or unintentionally—perhaps they will even jeer at you—why should you not go to Jesus who is your best friend?

Why should you not tell him all your troubles and worries?

Unite them to those which he himself suffered when he was here on earth; abandon yourself to him, convinced that he will be pleased to accept those sacrifices in reparation for your sins. Remember that such strength flows out from Jesus as can heal all wounds.

There are certain things, too, which should be told only to Jesus and to the man who represents him on earth and who has the direction of your soul. This does not mean that you cannot open your heart very often to some discreet and loyal friend. The Lord himself confided in his apostles when his soul was sad 'even unto death.' You can, then, open wide your heart, provided that deep down in your soul, in the supreme and most delicate point of your spirit, you make an act of resignation, of acceptance and of abandonment to the will of God.

What you must not do is to go and beg of creatures that which they cannot give. Each time we do this we are enervated and weakened, our heart feels even emptier.

EFFECTS OF HOLY COMMUNION

It is worth noting that 'the ignorance of many and their inability to comprehend the full extent of the action of this sacrament and the divine benefits which it confers, often make them consider a Communion to be less fruitful, simply because their feelings are not aroused or moved during the thanksgiving. They forget that the holy Eucharist is a mystery of faith, not only in regard to the real presence of our Lord hidden under the appearance of the host, but also in regard to the effects which the sacrament produces in the depths of our soul.'[21]

A mystery of Faith! Each holy Communion, well received, brings us closer to Christ, our Model; it makes us penetrate more intimately into the knowledge, love and practice of the mystery of our predestination and adoption in Jesus Christ, our eldest brother; it perfects in us the grace of divine filiation.

This notion is so important that I intend to insist on it. The whole of our sanctity consists in the participation, through grace, of the divine filiation of Jesus Christ; in the fact that we are, through our supernatural adoption, what Christ is by his nature: sons of God. The more intimate that participation, the more elevated is our sanctity. Now, what is it that confers upon us that participation, what is it that makes us sons of God? Saint John answers: It is the faith with which we receive Christ, fount and source of all grace (John I, 12). Therefore, the deeper our faith when we receive Jesus Christ, the more he communicates to us the greatest thing he has: his divine sonship; that is to say: the more we believe when we receive Communion, the greater is the extent of our participation in Christ's divine filiation.

Now, 'there is no action wherein our faith can be exercised with greater intensity than in Communion; there is no more sublime homage of faith than to believe in Christ

---

21 Cf. D. I Ryelandt: *Pour mieux communier,* Namur, 1927.

whose Divinity and Humanity are both hidden under the appearance of the host.'[22]

This first effect of holy Communion is an increase of sanctifying grace and the virtue of charity. The increase of sanctifying grace is produced in silence, as an effect of the sacrament.

The first effect, consists in the intensification and increase of the divine life in us, and there is manifested also the power which the Eucharist has to give us a *pledge of eternal life*.

The second effect is to enkindle in us, and make us practise, a deep love. That is so because the special end of the sacrament of the Eucharist is to unite the Christian spiritually, but really, to Christ and to God.

And since love is nourished by union, it is increased by the reception of the blessed Eucharist. Man must be united with God by means of human acts, spontaneous and deliberate. Now, the efforts which we make to become one with God must not consist solely in acts of *affective* love, such as delighting in the power of him whom we love, but must be of a more concrete and practical nature: correction of some defect, forgiveness of some injury done to us, reparation for some injury we have done or acceptance of some cross sent to us.

Another effect of the Eucharist is spiritual joy: the heavenly Bread contains all possible delights.

It is true that interior consolation is not always shared in the same degree by all the faithful, for everyone knows that very often, and not, indeed, through our own fault, we feel cold and dry. However our holy Communion is not less fruitful on that account.

What, then, is this gift of spiritual joy?

As a scholastic doctor of the Middle Ages said: 'Even if we do not always *feel* the sweetness of the Lord's presence... nevertheless we can *taste* it because we understand the immense usefulness of the sacrament.'

[22] D. Marmion: *Christ the Life of the Soul*, p. 278.

God can give us a deep understanding of the importance of this sacrament; and if we appreciate the divine gift properly we shall derive from the driest of Communions a deep comfort and happiness.

Finally, let us not forget that the Eucharist is 'a safeguard for our soul and body.' Let us, then, receive holy Communion, whenever possible, during holy Mass. Let us receive it every day.

Let us receive it, convinced that the presence of Christ in our souls gives us life, not only because it enlivens the deepest corners of our being, but also because it awakens in us lively sentiments of charity.

And let us not forget that this is 'the fruit properly belonging to the Eucharist: the identification of ourselves, through faith and love with Christ.'[23]

My friend, when you receive Christ into your soul, you must resemble him outwardly as well.

As Saint Augustine says, if you receive the body of Christ well, you will become him whom you receive.[24]

The fact is that 'One who claims to dwell in him must needs live and move as he lived and moved' (I Jn. II, 6).

Communion! Union of thoughts and sentiments. Passion and crucifixion first: ascension and glory afterwards.

So it is with us also: exile and suffering first, and only afterwards comes the promised happiness. The cross is the way to light. The *via dolorosa* is the way to heaven.

But do not see only sweetness in your Communion; you will find no real comfort, no lasting comfort, until you have drained the chalice...

You must resemble him...

Yes, my friend, and especially by being careful to avoid faults against charity. These are almost always the result of not living the great truth: that he who offends his neighbour

---

23   D. Marmion: *Christ the Life of the Soul*, p. 281.
24   *Sermo* LVII, C. 7.

in any way, offends Christ himself. And it is a grave fault against faith not to see Christ in our neighbour. If we were well permeated with this spirit of faith how many faults would we not avoid, how much more would we not respect those temples of the Lord, our own soul and the souls of our brothers.[25] How great is the excellence of souls, in which the Lord dwells, in which he prolongs his sacrifice, his passion and suffering!

Do you really desire to be united to the divine Spouse? If so remember that if a soul offends against charity and receives Christ in Communion, it cannot say to him: 'My Jesus, I love you with all my heart.' That would be a lie, because that soul does not embrace Christ and his members in the same love. That soul does not accept the mystery of the Incarnation in its totality. It stops at the individual humanity of Christ, and forgets that spiritual extension of the Incarnation, which is Christ's mystical Body. So that when we receive holy Communion we must be ready to embrace Christ and everything united to him, in the same charity; because—and take note of this—Jesus gives himself to our souls in the same measure and to the same extent as we give ourselves to our brothers.

Charity! But it may take many forms.
This is something very well understood by Isabel Leseur. She writes:[26] Fanaticism inspires me with an invincible horror, and I cannot see how it can go hand in hand with sincere

---

25 'The soul is so closely united to the body, there is such a substantial union between these two elements, that holy Communion as well as raising the soul to the heights of divine love, mitigates the flames of concupiscence, and weakens the appetite for sensible and vain pleasures. The Church very often asks in her Postcommunions that "through our participation in this Mystery thou wouldst teach us to despise earthly things and to love heavenly ones".' D. Marmion: *Sponsa Verbi*, CH. VI, cf. Postcommunions of 2nd Sunday of Advent and 4th Sunday after Epiphany.

26 *Pensées de chaque jour*, Paris 1927, p. 274

conviction. Anyone who loves Christianity passionately, and truly desires to see it reign in men's souls, how can he dream for a moment of using for this end any means other than persuasion? . . . How many little acts of fanaticism we commit without realising it! We lack personal pride, and have instead the pride of our faith, which is the most treacherous of all. With extraordinary serenity of conscience we despise those whose beliefs are different from our own, and we almost think we are exempt from exercising towards them the great law of charity. A Jew, a Protestant, an atheist, we scarcely look on as brothers, in the true sense of the word, brothers whom we love deeply, for whom we sacrifice ourselves and on whom we bestow our love with great delicacy. We seem to think that everything is permitted against them, even slander; and our object seems to be, not to convince, but to offend them.'

Since charity is the queen of all virtues even truth has to follow its directives. And although it is charity to correct those who are in error, still it is not charity vainly to pour bitter vinegar into open wounds. 'I do not say that we should hide the truth; what we should never do, however, is to separate the truth from charity.'[27]

This is all very important, for we may have many talents, many virtues, but they are all worth *nothing*, as Saint Paul tells us, without charity. *Nothing!* Let us remember that.

We have said that Jesus gives himself to our souls to the same extent as we give ourselves to our brothers. That much refers to this life.

And in the next life? Listen: our enjoyment of God in the next life will be in direct proportion to the use we make of his grace in this (cf. I Cor. III, 8).

'Do not let us lose sight of this truth: the degree of our eternal beatitude is and will remain fixed for ever by the degree of charity we shall have attained, by the grace of

---

[27] D. I, Van Houtryve: *A Vida na Paz*, p. 94.

Christ, when God shall call us to Himself. Each moment of our life, then, is infinitely precious, for it suffices to advance us a degree in the love of God, to raise us higher in the beatitude of eternal life.

'And let us not say that one degree more or less is a small matter. How can anything be a small matter when it concerns God, and the endless life and beatitude of which He is the source? If, according to the parable spoken by our Lord in person, we have received five talents, it was not that we might bury them, but that we might make them bear increase.'[28]

My friend, always avoid bitterness. Hate no man. 'Make peace with an adversary before the sun sets.'[29]

For God's sake do not say: To forgive offenses shows weakness! Consider well this prayer: 'O God who does manifest thy almighty power chiefly — *maxime* — in showing mercy and pity...'[30]

Saint Vincent de Paul says that 'God is a perpetual Communion for the soul that does his will.'

My friend, whenever the will of God points in a direction contrary to that in which you have been travelling and into which you put maybe your whole effort, then leave that way and follow the new. You will have the happiness of knowing certainly that the will of God is always the best for us. And since there is no distinction between the will of God and God himself, to fulfill that most sacred will is to communicate.

How often, even though we are quite sure that we are doing everything possible on our part — as much as in our power, weak and miserable as we are — our Lord still refuses to

---

[28] D. Marmion: *Christ the Life of the Soul*, p. 365.
[29] *Rule of St. Benedict*, Ch. IV, 71.
[30] Collect of the 10th Sunday after Pentecost.

show himself to us; on the contrary, all is cold, dry and unbearable, as if he were persecuting us!

And our soul feels restless and upset, like the uneasiness felt by one who is enormously thirsty and whose tongue sticks to his parched mouth.

In those moments only the most noble and most delicate extremity of our spirit remains united to the will of God, and in the middle of all the disturbance it is quite unaware that it does remain united to it. 'The soul makes this resignation amidst such a world of troubles, contradictions, repugnances that she hardly even perceives that she makes it; at least it seems done so coldly as not to be done from her heart nor properly, since what then goes on for the divine good pleasure is not only done without delight and contentment, but even against the pleasure and liking of all the rest of the heart.

'But this submissive peace is not tender or sweet, it is scarcely sensible, though sincere, strong, unchangeable and full of love.' But remember this: 'The more love is deprived of all helps and cut off from the aid of the powers and faculties of the soul, the more it is esteemed for preserving its fidelity so constantly.'

The love we show by voluntary mortification of body and mind is very pleasing to God, but 'it is still more so when we receive sweetly and contentedly, pains, torments and tribulations by reason of the divine will which sends them to us.'[31]

'Yes,' you say, 'I put all my energy into progressing in virtue and I do not see the fruit of my efforts.'

Look, my friend, the fault is yours. Be humble, ask the Lord's pardon and make a firm resolution to amend your life. But never become sad or upset.

Let your resolution to amend your life be firm, but calm.

---

31   St. Francis de Sales: *Treatise on the Love of God*, Bk. III, ch. 3.

If the fault is not yours, if your conscience tells you that you have done everything within your power to advance in virtue, and if you still see no progress, then remember that only God can give fruits. Trust in him to produce them.

Put yourself in his hands with the same blind confidence with which you once abandoned yourself in the arms of your mother. But I repeat: never get upset.

There are times, it is true, when it is difficult not to be gloomy and troubled. How many sincere and firm resolutions do we make never more to commit this fault or that, and nevertheless we find ourselves completely overcome by the first stirrings of that very passion.

But look, if we become upset in those cases, it is because we forget that those stirrings are only temptations and not sins: temptation can be in the feelings but sin is only in consent. Fundamentally it is our pride which causes that undesirable disturbance: it wants us to be free from all restraint.

Saint Paul — he who was the object of the very highest heavenly gifts — was very strongly moved by the sting of the flesh, and he asked the Lord to deliver him from that sting. But the Lord answered him: Paul, 'my grace is enough for thee; my strength finds its full scope in thy weakness' (II Cor. XII, 9).

Have recourse, like Saint Paul, to the great weapon of prayer, in the fight against these temptations. 'Note further that our Lord does not always permit these terrible revolts in man for the punishment of sin, but to manifest the strength and virtue of the divine assistance and grace. Finally, note that we are not only not to be disquieted in our temptations and infirmities, but we are even to glory in our infirmity that thereby God's virtue may appear in us, sustaining our weakness against the force of the suggestion and temptation.

'The Church condemned the error of certain solitaries, who held that we might be perfectly delivered even in this world from the passions of anger, concupiscence, fear and the like.'[32]

---

32 St. Francis de Sales: *Treatise on the Love of God*, Bk. IX, ch. 8.

'Carry God about in your bodies.'

Accept everything he sends you, absolutely everything.

Very often he bestows on his loved ones the favour of persecuting them with his love, of making their lives similar to his own painful Passion, of making them hosts like himself! We know well that the principal virtue of love is that the lover is made to suffer for the thing he loves.

There are souls of whom God asks many things, countless things. A saintly soul of our own times says—and speaking from his own experience—that 'when Love penetrates a generous soul it demands everything: first one thing, then another and another, until the soul is completely exhausted. It then feels the full weight of its absolute powerlessness, but begins to feel itself strong in God.'[33]

Sometimes God himself chooses these hosts, without their ever having envisaged such a thing. At other times he does no more than accept, literally, an offering made to him in some solemn moment of one's life.

And we are weak that, even if we make our vows to God with the best of intentions, in the moment of difficulty when the Lord asks us to do some of the things we promised, we try to escape. It cannot be denied that 'everyone deems himself able to drink our Saviour's chalice with him, but when it is in fact presented to us, we fly, we give up. Things proposed in detail make a more strong impression on our soul, and more sensibly wound the imagination. For this reason ... after general affections we should descend to particular resolutions in holy prayer.'[34]

A certain saint says there is no surer sign of love than a desire to suffer and feel pain. And it is true that in love of afflictions there is nothing to be loved, nothing, but the divine will.

Saint Paul, burning with a most pure love, cried out: 'God forbid that I should glory, save in the cross of our Lord Jesus Christ.'

33 D. P. d'Hemptine: *O Segredo do Claustro*, Braga.
34 St. Francis de Sales: *Treatise on the Love of God*, Bk. VIII, ch. 4.

God often hides from us. And then we have to advance like blind men feeling their way, like a little child learning to walk when its mother lets go its hand for the first time.

At times, my friend, it is our own fault: we offend against charity, frequently perhaps, and our offences, in our own eyes, seem to be nothing at all; our pride tries to justify them as best it can, but they are in fact very grave faults, all the graver the nearer we are to the Lord. And remember: to hurt one of his members is to hurt God himself.

'God often leaves you alone, that you may cultivate that humility which is proper to your weakness: that you may not despise others and may desire God himself more ardently; that you may pray more fervently and advance with more perseverance towards that eternal city where you will enjoy him for ever.'[35]

There are some people who love God so long as he gives them sensible consolations, but who change completely the moment he seems to leave them. These people, as Saint Francis de Sales says, would leave the love and offer up the sweetness if it could be separated from the love; they seek love for its joys, with little interest in the love itself. Those who act in this way, run a great risk — that of abandoning God when his joys and consolations leave them. They are distracted by vain joys, which are very different from genuine love.

'O souls that seek to walk in security and comfort! If ye did not know how necessary it is to suffer and endure in order to reach the lofty state, and of what great benefit it is to suffer and be mortified in order to reach such lofty blessings, ye would in no way seek consolation, either from God or from creatures.'[36]

---

35 D. Van Houtryve: *A Vida na Paz*, p. 116.
36 St. John of the Cross: *Living flame of love*, Stanza II, 24.

XIII
Thanksgiving

THE PRIEST'S THANKSGIVING BEGINS WHEN HE HAS received the body of Christ. He takes some verses from the psalms which the Lord recited at the last supper and says very slowly: 'What shall I render to the Lord for all the things that he hath rendered to me?'

Indeed, poor man, what can he render to God when all he has is nothing and less than nothing? And the abyss between nothingness and everything is so great!

But Christ is the Way.

And the priest then takes in his hands, in his most unworthy hands, the 'chalice of salvation' invoking and proclaiming the name of the Lord: 'I shall receive the chalice of salvation and call upon the name of the Lord.'

The chalice is thus the expression of his gratitude, that is to say: only Jesus is his own praise and his own act of thanksgiving, because only he is truly a priest and truly a host: he is the Word made flesh, the herald, above all others, of the glory of his Father.

The priest then drinks the blood of the Lord, expressing a sincere wish that it may preserve his soul for eternal life.

Then, while the wine is being poured into the chalice, he continues his act of thanksgiving: 'Grant, O Lord, that what we have taken with our mouth, we may receive with a pure mind: and that from a temporal gift it may become for us an eternal remedy.'

After that, while he is purifying his fingers over the chalice, with wine and water, he prays: 'May thy body, O Lord, which I have received, and thy blood which I have drunk, cleave to my inmost parts, and grant that no stain of sin may remain in me, whom these pure and holy sacraments have refreshed.'

Very often the Postcommunion also expresses this same sentiment of immense gratitude. In one of these prayers[1] we even pray that we may spend the whole of our life in a perpetual act of thanksgiving, in perpetual praise.

If only we did that!

And why should we not? It is so easy! The only thing necessary is that there should be perfect conformity between what we say we are and what we are in fact: Christians, other Christs.

And yet, we are so very far from being what we should be. 'Do not let us, from want of generosity, and in order to excuse our sloth, say that we are weak. This is true, more true even than we think. But by the side of this abyss (it is one) of our weakness, which is, however, compatible with our good will — and our Lord knows this good will better than we do — there is another abyss, that of the merits and treasures of Christ; and, by Communion, this Christ is ours.'[2]

BEFORE TURNING TO BLESS THE PEOPLE, THE PRIEST announces the end of Mass. And the people answer him with an expression of acknowledgement, an act of thanksgiving: *Deo gratias*, thanks be to God. Sometimes, too, the priest invites the people to give thanks to the Lord, to bless him: *Benedicamus Domino*, let us bless the Lord. This *Deo gratias* is repeated at the end of the last Gospel and brings to an end all the public liturgy.

Then the priest begins that beautiful canticle of thanksgiving, the *Benedicite*.

AND WHAT ABOUT THE FAITHFUL?

Why should they not give thanks like the priest and with the priest? Why should they not make use of his voice to

---

[1] Grant, we beseech thee, O Lord, that being replenish with holy gifts, we may ever prolong our thanksgiving for them.' (Sunday after the Octave of the Ascension.)
[2] D. Marmion: *Christ the Life of the Soul*, p. 282.

speak to his Spouse? Why should they not proclaim their love with these words, so old and yet so new?

IT IS A WIDELY-HELD DOCTRINE IN THE HOLY Church that the Sacred species remain for about a quarter of an hour after being consumed. That, at least, should be the period of our thanksgiving after holy Communion.

Somebody has said that if you see your priest make his thanksgiving very distractedly and hurriedly, even though he has no grave reason for his haste, no necessary, indispensable and urgent business, or if it happens — as may God forbid — that he makes no act of thanksgiving at all, then you must pray for him very much to the Lord, because that contributed to his agony...

The same can be said of any member of the faithful...

It is so sad to see that many souls, who could be temples of God, are miserable sepulchres.

IT IS RECOMMENDED THAT OUR THANKSGIVING should be in accordance with the spirit of the Communion or Postcommunion or of the Mass in general. Thus the taste of our daily bread will vary from one Mass to another: today sacrifice, always affective and especially *effective* love. Now, love is nourished, in fact it lives, by union: union of sentiments, of thoughts, of deeds.

Saint Augustine says: 'If you receive the body of Christ well, you will be what you receive': Christians, other Christs.

DO YOU WISH TO PROLONG YOUR THANKSGIVING? It may be, indeed, that the divine inspiration urges you to prolong your conversation with God. If you can do it without detriment to the duties of your profession—but they come first—then do so by all means. How? In any way you like. The holy Ghost will guide you as to what is the most suitable way. 'The one thing necessary is that we should recognise the greatness of the divine gift which Saint Paul declares to be "unspeakable", and that we should draw, for our own needs and those of our brothers and of the whole Church, from this infinite treasury.'[3]

DO YOU THINK IT IMPOSSIBLE, IN THE MIDDLE OF the affairs and bustle of the world, to raise up your heart to God, from time to time, for an instant, but with great affection? Remember: if your soul is in the state of grace, everything you do is a prayer.

That is to say: if your actions are in keeping with your dignity as a free and rational creature, as a son of God, they will all give thanks to God, all your life will be a prayer, your days will be filled with perpetual praise.

And you will thus be preparing for a new friendship, more and more intimate, with the divine Spouse, and for a never-ending communion with him in heaven.

THANKSGIVING: ALWAYS AND FOR EVERYTHING. LET your soul, detached from itself, completely abandoned to the holy will of God, give thanks always, for prosperity and for adversity, for health and for illness, for fervour and for interior dryness. Then it will be filled with a peace which nothing can disturb; indeed how could it be troubled, for it no longer lives but Christ lives in it?

The beginning, of course, is difficult. But the generous soul opens its gates to the outpourings of grace, and begins to get free of itself little by little, until it attains such a love of God that all fear vanishes. Then it begins to taste real happiness on its journey and to do everything, no longer for fear of punishment, but for love of Christ, encouraged by the delights which it feels in the practice of virtue.[4]

And now delay no longer. Run, very quickly, on the way of the Lord.

---

[3] D. Marmion: *Christ the Life of the Soul*, p. 281.
[4] Cf. *Rule of St. Benedict*, ch. VII.

ABOUT THE AUTHOR

BERNARDO VAZ LOBO TEIXEIRA DE VASCONCELOS, born on July 7, 1902 at S. Romao de Corgo, Portugal, entered the Order of St. Benedict in 1924, made his profession on September 29, 1925, and received the minor orders on the 5th and 6th of January 1929. His greatest desire was to be ordained to the priesthood and offer the Holy Sacrifice. But this desire was never to see fulfilment. Instead, the young monk was to spend the last six years of his life constantly tortured by illness and great physical suffering. Several very painful operations left his body covered with wounds but could do little to alleviate the excruciating pain, which remained with him until his death on July 4, 1932. *The Mass & The Interior Life* (*A Missa e a Vida Interior*) was partly written and partly dictated in the middle of this unrespited agony.

www.ingramcontent.com/pod-product-compliance
Lightning Source LLC
Chambersburg PA
CBHW021428070526
44577CB00001B/114

ABOUT THE AUTHOR

BERNARDO VAZ LOBO TEIXEIRA DE VASCONCELOS, born on July 7, 1902 at S. Romao de Corgo, Portugal, entered the Order of St. Benedict in 1924, made his profession on September 29, 1925, and received the minor orders on the 5th and 6th of January 1929. His greatest desire was to be ordained to the priesthood and offer the Holy Sacrifice. But this desire was never to see fulfilment. Instead, the young monk was to spend the last six years of his life constantly tortured by illness and great physical suffering. Several very painful operations left his body covered with wounds but could do little to alleviate the excruciating pain, which remained with him until his death on July 4, 1932. *The Mass & The Interior Life* (*A Missa e a Vida Interior*) was partly written and partly dictated in the middle of this unrespited agony.

declares to be "unspeakable", and that we should draw, for our own needs and those of our brothers and of the whole Church, from this infinite treasury.'[3]

DO YOU THINK IT IMPOSSIBLE, IN THE MIDDLE OF the affairs and bustle of the world, to raise up your heart to God, from time to time, for an instant, but with great affection? Remember: if your soul is in the state of grace, everything you do is a prayer.

That is to say: if your actions are in keeping with your dignity as a free and rational creature, as a son of God, they will all give thanks to God, all your life will be a prayer, your days will be filled with perpetual praise.

And you will thus be preparing for a new friendship, more and more intimate, with the divine Spouse, and for a never-ending communion with him in heaven.

THANKSGIVING: ALWAYS AND FOR EVERYTHING. LET your soul, detached from itself, completely abandoned to the holy will of God, give thanks always, for prosperity and for adversity, for health and for illness, for fervour and for interior dryness. Then it will be filled with a peace which nothing can disturb; indeed how could it be troubled, for it no longer lives but Christ lives in it?

The beginning, of course, is difficult. But the generous soul opens its gates to the outpourings of grace, and begins to get free of itself little by little, until it attains such a love of God that all fear vanishes. Then it begins to taste real happiness on its journey and to do everything, no longer for fear of punishment, but for love of Christ, encouraged by the delights which it feels in the practice of virtue.[4]

And now delay no longer. Run, very quickly, on the way of the Lord.

---

3 D. Marmion: *Christ the Life of the Soul*, p. 281.
4 Cf. *Rule of St. Benedict*, ch. VII.

speak to his Spouse? Why should they not proclaim their love with these words, so old and yet so new?

IT IS A WIDELY-HELD DOCTRINE IN THE HOLY Church that the Sacred species remain for about a quarter of an hour after being consumed. That, at least, should be the period of our thanksgiving after holy Communion.

Somebody has said that if you see your priest make his thanksgiving very distractedly and hurriedly, even though he has no grave reason for his haste, no necessary, indispensable and urgent business, or if it happens — as may God forbid — that he makes no act of thanksgiving at all, then you must pray for him very much to the Lord, because that contributed to his agony...

The same can be said of any member of the faithful...

It is so sad to see that many souls, who could be temples of God, are miserable sepulchres.

IT IS RECOMMENDED THAT OUR THANKSGIVING should be in accordance with the spirit of the Communion or Postcommunion or of the Mass in general. Thus the taste of our daily bread will vary from one Mass to another: today sacrifice, always affective and especially *effective* love. Now, love is nourished, in fact it lives, by union: union of sentiments, of thoughts, of deeds.

Saint Augustine says: 'If you receive the body of Christ well, you will be what you receive': Christians, other Christs.

DO YOU WISH TO PROLONG YOUR THANKSGIVING? It may be, indeed, that the divine inspiration urges you to prolong your conversation with God. If you can do it without detriment to the duties of your profession—but they come first—then do so by all means. How? In any way you like. The holy Ghost will guide you as to what is the most suitable way. 'The one thing necessary is that we should recognise the greatness of the divine gift which Saint Paul

Thanksgiving

WHEN WILL YOU BEGIN? REMEMBER: YOU CAN DO all things in him who strengthens you, and it is through him, with him and in him, that all glory is given to God the Father in the unity of the holy Ghost.